ROLE OF WAREHOUSES IN INDIAN ECONOMY

ROLE OF WAREHOUSES IN INDIAN ECONOMY

Prasanna Kumar Mishra
Devi Prasad Misra

PUBLICATIONS

KALPAZ PUBLICATIONS
DELHI - 110052

Role of Warehouses in Indian Economy

Rs. 790

ISBN: 81-7835-348-2

Published in 2005 in India by
Kalpaz Publications
C-30, Satyawati Nagar
Delhi-110052
e-mail: kalpaz@hotmail.com

Laser Typeset at: Alphabet, Delhi
Printed at: Mehra Offset Press, Delhi

Dedicated to
my father
Late Ramesh Chandra Mishra

Contents

Shri Ramesh Ch. Behera I.A.S.,
Commissioner-cum-Secretary to Govt.
Department of Higher Education,
Orissa

Foreword

Warehousing plays an important role in our economy by providing scientific storage facilities to prevent losses in storage, assisting in the expansion of institutional credit to the farmers and small traders and preventing distress sale immediately after harvest at prevailing low price. Little literature is available on the subject. This piece of work would definitely enrich the literature on warehousing business in India.

The book discusses in detail the performance of OSWC with regard to physical, financial and human resources. These aspects are presented in a simple, lucid and precise manner.

I hope this book will be of immense help to a wide section of readers particularly the OSWC which could improve the performance by adopting the valuable suggestions provided in the book.

Bhubaneswar
Dated: 8.10.04

R.C. Behera

Shri Dandanirodha Mishra, I.A.S.
Commissioner-cum-Secretary to Government
Department of Labour and Employment
Orissa

Message

Public Warehousing in Orissa, with its steady progress over last 45 years, has contributed significantly to the economic growth of the State especially in the agricultural sector. The contribution of the Orissa State Warehousing Corporation, singularly, in this regard can be considered to be simply outstanding.

During my tenure as Managing Director of Orissa State Warehousing Corporation (OSWC), I came to know Dr. P.K. Mishra whose research work under the title "A Critical Analysis on the Working of the OSWC" helped me a lot to know the history, the development and the objectives of OSWC. This research book describes different aspects on the working of the OSWC in relation to its physical and financial performances in a lucid manner with in-depth analysis. Dr Mishra's evaluation of financial data with specific relation to analysis of different ratios is praiseworthy.

I hope, this book will be of great help to the researchers and managers by providing a new insight in the field of warehousing.

D. Mishra
19/11/2004

Dated: 19.11.2004
Bhubaneswar

(Dandanirodha Mishra)

Preface

Agriculture is the back-bone of the Indian economy which contributes a major share of the national income. Being an agrarian country nearly 75 per cent of the country's population depend directly or indirectly on agriculture. Due to successful research and extension in agriculture, there has been a phenomenal growth in the production. The production of foodgrains increased from 50.8 million tonnes in 1950-51, i.e., beginning of the First Five Year Plan to 209 million tonnes by the end of 1999-2000. In order to cope up with the increase in production there is necessity for an effective food management system in the country.

The concept of public warehousing in India is the outcome of the recommendations made by the Royal Commission on Agriculture in 1928, Agriculture Finance Sub-Committee in 1944 and All India Rural Credit Survey Committee set up by the Reserve Bank of India in 1954. Finally, in 1956, the Parliament enacted the Agricultural Produce (Development and Warehousing) Corporations Act, 1956. Accordingly, the Central Warehousing Corporation was set up in 1957 and 16 State Warehousing Corporations were established thereafter. This Act was subsequently repealed and replaced by the Warehousing Corporations Act, 1962 in the thirteenth year of the Republic of India.

The main objectives of setting up of Warehousing Corporations in India are to prevent distress sale immediately after harvest at prevailing low prices, to provide scientific storage facilities to prevent losses in storage and assist in expanding institutional credit to the farmers. The Orissa State Warehousing Corporation started functioning in the state during 1958. Over a period of years the OSWC has been providing infrastructural facilities for scientific storage of agricultural produce and other notified commodities and also assisting State Government in implementing its plans, programmes and policies meant for the people of Orissa more particularly for the rural massess.

Keeping in view the importance of warehousing system and the role played by the OSWC in the development of the economy of Orissa, this piece of research work is undertaken to assess the overall strength and weakness of the Orissa State Warehousing Corporation.

The data for the study have been collected from the Annual Reports of the OSWC, the CWC and 16 State Warehousing Corporations for the period from 1985-86 to 1999-2000. The data collected from the financial statements is analysed with the help of important financial techniques, like trend analysis and ratio analysis. The strength and weakness of the OSWC with regard to its physical, financial and human resource aspects are studied. That apart statistical techniques such as mean, standard deviation, co-efficient of variation and correlation analysis are used to provide a more scientific analysis for the present study.

Prasanna Kumar Mishra

Devi Prasad Misra

Abbreviations

ACC	Air Cargo Complexes.
CAGR	Compounded Average Growth Rate.
CARE	Co-operative for American Relief Everywhere.
CF Ltd.	Coromondel Fertilizers Limited.
CFC	Container Freight Station.
CV	Coefficient of Variation.
CWC	Central Warehousing Corporation.
DESS	Disinfestation Extension Service Scheme.
DMC Ltd.	Dharamsi Morarjee and Chemicals Cooperative Limited.
DPS	Dividend Per Share.
EBIT	Earnings Before Interest and Taxes.
EPS	Earnings Per Share.
FCI	Food Corporation of India.
FCI Ltd.	Fertilizer Corporation of India Limited.
FESS	Farmers Extension Service Scheme.
GSFertilizer	Gouri Shankar Fertilizers Private Limited.
HI Ltd.	Hindustan Insecticides Limited.
IFFCO	Indian Farmers Fertilizer Co-operative Limited.
IP Ltd.	Indian Potash Limited.
KRIBHCO	Krishi Bharati Co-operative Limited.
MARKFED	Orissa State Co-operative Marketing Federation Ltd.

MMTC	Minerals and Metals Trading Corporation Limited.
MT	Metric Tonne.
NAFED	National Agricultural Co-operative Marketing Federation of India Limited.
NCDC	National Co-operative Development Corporation.
NF Ltd.	National Fertilizers Limited.
NFC Ltd.	Nagarjun Fertilizer and Chemical Limited.
NMEP	National Malaria Eradication Programme.
OFDC	Orissa Forest Development Corporation.
OPOLFED	Orissa Poultry Federation.
OSWC	Orissa State Warehousing Corporation.
PDS	Public Distribution System.
PP Ch Ltd.	Pyrites Phosphates and Chemicals Limited.
PP Ltd.	Paradeep Phosphates Limited.
RCF Ltd.	Rastriya Chemicals and Fertilizers Limited.
ROA	Return on Assets.
ROCE	Retun on Capital Employed.
ROI	Return on Investment.
RP Agrochemical	Rhone Poulenc Agrochemicals (India) Limited.
SD	Standard Deviation.
SEWA	Social Enrichment Workers' Association.
SWC	State Warehousing Corporation.
SWOT	Strength, Weakness, Opportunities and Threats
TDCC	Tribal Development Co-operative Corporation.
TRIFED	Tribal Co-operative Marketing Development Federation of India Ltd.

List of Figures and Tables

One

Introduction and Methodology

Importance of Warehousing

Agriculture provides an important source of income in India where bulk of the population depends directly or indirectly on a broad spectrum of agricultural activities. Over the years, the country witnessed a historic change-over from a subsistence agricultural production to market oriented surplus. This is possible due to modern technologies applied to agriculture that in fact enhanced the momentum of foodgrains production. Today agricultural sector occupies a strategic place in India's economic development as it provides livelihood to about 75 per cent of country's population. Besides, it employs over 74 per cent of the work force and contributes about 42 per cent to the national income.[1] The production of foodgrains increased considerably from 50.8 million tonnes in 1950-51, i.e., beginning of the First Five Year Plan to an all time record of 209 million tonnes by the end of 1999-2000.

However, for a long period of time Indian agriculture was mostly in the nature of 'subsistence farming'. The farmers sold only a small part of their produce to payoff rents, debts and meet other requirements. Such sale was usually done immediately after harvesting of crops since there were no storing facilities. A major portion of the total produce was sold by the farmers to the village traders and money lenders often at prices much lower than the market prices through middlemen. As a result, the return from agricultural produce to farmers was meagre. For instance, a study made by D.S. Sidhu has revealed that farmers obtain only about 53 per cent of the price of rice, 31 per cent being the share of middlemen and the remaining 16 per cent being the market cost[2].

In addition to the above defects in the agricultural marketing system in India, there were various other problems including the presence of large number of middlemen and the prevalence of widespread malpractices in the *mandis*. For instance, there was absence of proper warehousing facilities in the villages. As a consequence, the farmer was compelled to store his produce in pits, mud-vessels and traditional store houses. These unscientific methods of storing led to considerable wastage. While some parts of the produce were used to get rotten and unfit for human consumption, few other parts were eaten away by pests and rodents. At times, as much as one third of farmers' produce was lost in this way. It was, therefore, felt that in order to avoid exploitation of producers by the traders, and to preserve the produce from the ravages of insects and pests during post-harvest period, the infrastructure of warehousing has to be taken to the rural areas. Likewise as stated earlier, due to record production of foodgrains in the recent times, the marketable surplus do pose a challenge to provide requisite storage and warehousing facilities for proper upkeep and distribution of the commodities. As such, storage of foodgrains is necessary to bridge the time gap between periodic harvest and marketing, and relatively stable consumption of food on a year round basis. Further, grain storage also adds value not only to the product but also serves as a buffer at the time of adversity.

To improve the conditions of agricultural marketing the Government of India has taken various steps during various Plan periods. It has set up the All India Warehousing Corporation to construct and manage a whole network of warehouses in all towns and *mandis* (wholesale market). The warehousing facilities are necessary to prevent the loss arising out of defective storage and also to equip the farmers with a convenient instrument of credit. Both the Agricultural Finance Sub-Committee (1945) and the Rural Banking Enquiry Committee (1950) emphasized the importance of warehousing as a method of promoting rural banking and finance in India. An important land mark in the field of warehousing was the recommendation of All India Rural Credit Survey Committee (1954) for initiating a countrywide programme of warehousing development. This Committee recommended a three-tier system at (a) the national level (b) state and district level (c) village and rural level. In accordance with its recommendations, the Food Corporation of India and the Central Warehousing Corporation were required to create storage facilities at centers of all-India importance; the State Governments were allowed to start State Warehousing Corporation's warehouses at centers of state/district level importance and the rural storage needs were to be looked after by the cooperatives. The Government of India accepted the recommendations of the Committee and set up the National Cooperative Development and Warehousing Board in 1956 and the Central Warehousing Corporation in 1957. This was followed by the setting up of State Warehousing Corporation by the States.

At present there are three main agencies in the public sector which are engaged in building large-scale storage/ warehouses. They are the Food Corporation of India (FCI), the Central Warehousing Corporation (CWC) and 16 State Warehousing Corporations (SWCs).

The main functions of the CWC and the SWCs are to acquire and build warehouses at suitable places and operate them for storage of agricultural produce, fertilizer and other notified commodities. The CWC owns and manages about 451 warehouses with a total capacity of 7.5 million tonnes. The number of warehouses owned and managed by State Warehousing Corporations (SWCs) are 1440 with a storage capacity of 12 million tonnes.

In 1960-61, there were only 40 general warehouses in the country with a total capacity of less than 0.1 million tonnes[3]. At present the three public sector units together have a storage capacity of 45 million tonnes. Apart from public sector agencies, cooperatives have also constructed warehouses in rural areas for storage of agricultural produce including fertilizer, consumer articles and other inputs of their members. To avoid unfair competition with the cooperative marketing societies, the State Warehousing Corporations do not open warehouses at any place below the sub-division level.

During Sixth and Seventh Plans, the Central Government had promoted a national programme of storage with a view to develop "a well-spread out storage grid from the farm to the national level". At the base the programme envisaged the construction of rural godowns each having a 100 MT capacity. Bulk of these rural godowns were in the cooperative sector. This was supplemented by a Rural Godowns Scheme which was centrally sponsored but implemented through Market Committees and State Warehousing Corporation. The objective was to build godowns of larger capacity of 200 to 1,000 MT in rural areas to facilitate storage of produce of small and marginal farmers.

To sum up, warehouses have two definite advantages: (i) to provide better and scientific storage facilities at a reasonable cost, and (ii) to provide farmers and traders with convenient instrument of credit in the form of warehouse receipt against which they can borrow money from the banks. In other words, warehouses are providing storage facilities at cheaper rates consistent with local requirements.

Need for Warehousing

In India, public warehousing has created a wide spread and well established network of godowns to support agriculture, industry and trade. It provides not only vast storage facilities to the notified commodities but also ensures regular supply of goods to ultimate consumers.

The objective of storing agricultural produce is to minimise the post harvest losses. With this objective in mind, we may have a look at the existing total storage capacity with the storage capacity available two decades ago. At the time of setting up of warehousing business in India on Scientific line, the responsibility of storage and construction of storage structures were assigned to the public sectors because of heavy amount of capital expenditure. Food Corporation of India (FCI), Central Warehousing Corporation (CWC) and State Warehousing Corporation (SWC) are the main public sector undertakings, which are actively engaged in offering storage services to the public. Out of these public sectors, FCI procures foodgrains from producers and also through miller agents. Warehousing Corporations, both Central and State, are engaging themselves in storing the produce of the persons who desire so, on payment of nominal storage charge. The Corporation issues a warehouse receipt which a farmer/ producer can pledge with a scheduled bank for availing loans. That apart, Warehousing Corporations are also accepting industrial commodities for storage as notified in the Warehousing Corporations Act, 1962.

The total production of foodgrains in 1999-2000 stood at 2088.7 lakh tonnes, while the storage capacity available during the said period was 645.21 lakh tonnes. The figures have indicated that only 30.89 per cent of total produce could be stored with the existing storage facilities. Further, many other agricultural produce like spices, oil seeds and forest products etc. have also been stored in the warehouses. Similarly, a portion of the warehouse has also been utilised for storage of other notified commodities. Taking all these aspects into consideration, it is believed that only 10 per cent of the total foodgrains production was being accommodated in the godowns of the Public Sector Undertakings.

The state-wise position of foodgrains production and storage capacity also reveals that there is a wide gap between these two. The gap will expand further, if other commodities accepted for storage are taken into consideration[4]. The data reveals that the foodgrains production has grown at an annual compound growth rate of 2.65 per cent from 1966-67 to 2000-2001. If foodgrains production grow at the same rate, the production would be 2526.77 lakh tonnes by the end of 2005. With the existing capacity (assuming that entire existing storage capacity would be utilised for foodgrains) only 25 per cent of the total production can be accommodated[5]. This reflects the growing need for warehousing in the coming days in order to accommodate the huge agricultural produce.

The need for increasing the storage capacity is emphasized when the foodgrains production alone is considered. However, the storage facilities are of greater importance for other industrial as well as perishable commodities. Further, there are instances where the producers are forced to sell their produce at a nominal price due to paucity of proper storage space. Therefore, arrangement for adequate storage facilities is the need of the hour. It will not only safeguard the interest of producers and consumers but also ensure smooth supply of goods.

Keeping in mind the need and importance of warehousing system and the role played by the OSWC in the development of economy of Orissa, this piece of study has been undertaken to assess the extent to which the OSWC has fulfilled its responsiblities.

Review of Literature

The review of literature on the subject, i.e., warehousing business would provide better insight into the diversified aspects of their workings. It would also provide the important findings of various empirical studies carried out so far in this area. In India no serious attempt has been made to study the performance of the Warehousing Corporations. However, the physical and financial performance of the Central Warehousing Corporation (CWC) is reviewed periodically by the Department of Food, Government of India. Apart from that, various Committees constituted by the Parliament such as, Estimate Committee, Committee on Public Undertakings, Public Accounts Committee have studied the performance of the Central Warehousing Corporation and recommended suggestions for improving the performance of the CWC. Besides the committees, a number of consultant agencies have also carried out some sort of review of the working of the CWC. The important among them are O and M unit of the Department of Food, Government of India, Indian Institute of Public Administration, New Delhi, National Productivity Council, New Delhi, Tata Economic Consultancy Services, Bombay and others. Most of the above Committees and Consultancy Organizations have studied the operational system of storage facilities, organizational study, establishment of cold storage, assessment of staff norms, warehousing and distribution etc. of the Central Warehousing Corporation. Besides these, there are few empirical studies on the working of State Warehousing Corporation. On the whole, there is scanty of literature for review. However, the findings of important Committees and few empirical studies are discussed below.

The Committee on Public Undertakings 1967-68 reviewed the working of the CWC in the light of the recommendation for winding up of the CWC. It recommended that there is a need to develop warehousing scheme by increasing the scope of operations of the CWC and centralize the warehousing operations in the country which are at present being carried out by different agencies. Further the Committee strongly recommended that the storage should be recognized as specialized function and handled by one agency. The Committee in its report further recommended that there should not be multiple agencies providing godown facilities at one place because it would be uneconomical to all of them.

The Committee on Public Undertakings 1973-74 in its report expressed the feeling that with the progress made in agricultural front in the country, the warehousing for storage of foodgrains and other commodities assumes greater importance. The committee expressed the view that there should be a close coordination between FCI, CWC and SWCs and such other organizations dealing with storage in order to avoid duplication in providing storage facilities. Further, the Committee suggested that the CWC should give a significant lead in developing storage facilities which are most modern and most competitive in rates for keeping refrigerated foods, fruits etc.

The Committee on Public Undertakings 1980-81 in its report recommended that it should be made mandatory for the public sector undertakings to make use of government owned warehouses wherever available. The Committee also observed that the CWC is the agency which can be broad based to ensure better utilization of storage capacity.

Besides the above reviews made by the various committees, a few researchers have also conducted studies on the working of Warehousing Corporations. The important empirical studies are discussed below.

Thomas presented in his study the waste and loss of foodgrains during storage, transport, process etc. He advocted an integrated approach consisting the basic elements such as construction of suitable storage structure with modern amenities for handling, weighing, cleaning, drying etc.; uniform grading of foodgrains; proper credit facilities; adquate provision for dunnage; proper stacking, quality control, better transportion, training and extension service, modern methods of processing etc. He remarked that if these basic elements are adequately taken care of, then the waste and loss on account of storage, transport and processing could be minimised substantially.[6]

Ram in his study on improvement of storage condtions and storage methods in India highlighted the wastage and loss of foodgrains during pre-storing and post-storing periods[7]. He emphasised that the 'Save Grain Campaign' launched by the Government must be implemented with letter and spirit. To achive this objective he highlighted the various services given by the government to farmers, traders, pest control firms, manufactures of storage bins, research institutions. He concluded that these services would enable them to join in this noble campaign to minimise the foodgrains wastages and losses.

Chhiber made an in-depth study on Warehousing Corporations in India with special reference to the CWC.[8] His study is an attempt to evaluate the working of the CWC. The study revealed the evolution and development of public warehousing along with the information and data relating to various disciplines of Central and State Warehousing Corporations. The study further pointed out the imperative need and importance of the creation of infrastructure of warehousing as an integral part of any project/programme of production, intra and inter state distribution of goods and foreign trade. It also brought home in clear and simple language, the relevance, significance and avantage of public warehousing as an industry.

Choyal made a study on the problems of pricing in the CWC. He made an elaborate analysis on the cost structure of the construction of storage space and its management[9]. He had also dealt with the financing aspect of the constructed project. Basing on cost benefit analysis he concluded that the service charges levied by the corporation are the bare minimum to cover its operational cost only. Further he concluded that in the matter of pricing policy, the corporation has been guided more by consideration on public interest rather than by profit motive.

A study on 'Warehousing and Distribution' with particular reference to Agro-Industrial Development was made by Sharma in late 80s[10]. His work was an attempt to highlight various important aspects of public warehousing and distribution system in India as well as abroad. The study dealt with the concept of warehousing as an economic activity, establishing linkages with marketing through the orderly processes of storage, transport and distribution. The study also highlighted on warehousing and distribution with related problems in terms of food economy/ agro-economy and other relevant aspects viz. productivity, transportation, consumerism, food policy, food security, food aid, demand growth, distribution channel and rural warehousing etc.

Ranganathan carried out a study on the performance of Tamil Nadu Warehousing Corporation[11]. He briefly dealt the objectives of the State Warehousing Corporation and its role in the State's economy. His study covered a period of 6 years i.e. from 1980-81 to 1985-86 with regard to the number of warehouses, its capacity and occupancy, income generated by the Corporation etc. Further, he highlighted the problems and prospects of Tamil Nadu Warehousing Corporation. In order to boost the warehousing activities in the state, he suggested a system of "warehouse on wheels". The system envisaged that a warehouse should be located within 10 kms. of railway station to enable the manufacturer or buyer to transport the product from the firm to the warehouses. This would help in minimising transportation cost and satisfying warehousing economy.

Gill, et. al. made a study on the storage losses of foodgrains at firm level in the state of Punjab[12]. The objectives of their study were to examine the type of storage structures used by the farmers and the extent of losses caused during storage at the firm level. They selected a total of 270 farmers drawn from different parts of the state by following purposive random sampling method. They collected information on the size of their operational holding, area under different foodgrains for rabi and kharif crops for the year 1980-81, quantity of foodgrains stored for family consumption and seed, storage structures used and the losses in each case. The study revealed that non-availability of separate godowns, poor type of storage structures, non-availability of dunnage etc. were the important causes for storage losses. They suggested few remedial measures to reduce the storage loss. These included construction of pucca godowns with dunnage facilities, inspection of godowns by the extension agencies and establishment of warehousing facilities in the villages.

Arora and Raju conducted a study on problems and prospects of rural godowns of Karnataka state[13]. They collected various information through structured questionnaire with regard to the rural godowns, the beneficiaries and non-beneficiaries and the implementing agencies. They observed that low capacity utilization, poor participation by farmers, misutilization of godowns, malfunctioning of godowns were the major failures in the functioning of rural godowns. They suggested that the farmers' participation is highly essential in order to improve the performance of rural godowns. Further, they also suggested that the basic amenities are to be provided in the rural godowns so as to make them viable and operational.

From the above review of literature, it is found that the Committees reviewed the working of the CWC and made certain suggestions for its improvement. Till date, no substantial work has been done on the working of the State Warehousing Corporations in general and OSWC in particular. In view of this, an attempt is made to study and examine the performance of the Orissa State Warehousing Corporation with regard to its commercial, financial and human resource utilization.

Methodology

The detailed methodology adopted for carrying out the present study is outlined below. The methodology discusses elaborately the objective and scope of the study, sources and collection of data, period of study and the techniques used for the study. Further, the hypotheses to be tested in the due course of the analysis are presented. The limitation of the study is also included in this section.

Objective of the Study

Given the immense importance of warehouses in the Indian economy particularly in the agriculture sector, it is felt necessary to examine the physical and financial performance of the Warehousing Corporations operating in storage and distribution of agricultural and allied produce. An attempt has been made to evaluate the performance of the Orissa State Warehousing Corporation and offer constructive suggestions for improving the performance of the organization.

Scope of the Study

The Orissa State Warehousing Corporation has been selected as a sample unit for the present study. So far as the storage/godown facilities is concerned, apart from OSWC, FCI and CWC are also providing such facilities in the state of Orissa. But the share of OSWC out of the total capacity of warehouses available in the state is 42%. Keeping this in view, the OSWC has been selected for the present study. The scope of the study is limited to the analysis of physical performance, financial performance and performance of manpower of the organization. In order to draw the conclusion, a number of mathematical, financial and statistical tools and techniques have been used in this study. The analysis has been carried out basically to know the strengths and weaknesses of the OSWC.

Sources of Data

The data for the present study has been collected mainly from secondary sources. For this, books, journals, periodicals and reports have been referred to collect the data and information on warehousing business. Further, the annual reports of the OSWC have been utilised to get the pertinent information on the physical, financial and manpower performance of the organization. Apart from these, an attempt has been made to collect the information from primary source i.e. direct interview with the field level executives to know the practical problems faced by them in the field level.

Period of the Study

The period for the present study covers 15 years from 1984-85 to 1999-2000. The significance of choosing the above period lies on the fact that during these years the agricultural production has marked a significant upward trend and the demand for storage facilities has grown at a rapid rate. Besides this, the government of India has started the liberalization programme since the early part of 1990s. This assumes significance because with the liberalization of the economy it is necessary to evaluate the performance of the OSWC during the post-liberalized period. This will help to make a comparative analysis on the performance of the OSWC during pre-liberalized era (1984-85 to 1990-91) with post-liberalized era (1991-92 to 1999-2000). Finally, for analyzing the trend, a period of 10 to 15 years is essential because it can provide better insight into the behaviour and pattern of growth or otherwise of the concerned unit.

Techniques of Analysis

The data collected from the financial statements of the sample unit is analysed with the help of financial techniques. The use and significance of the financial techniques applied in the present study are described below.

(i) Trend Analysis

Trend analysis makes it easy to understand the changes in an item or group of items over a period of time and to draw conclusion regarding its movement. For this purpose, a base year is chosen and the amount or number of an item in the base year is taken equal to one hundred and index numbers are calculated for other years on the basis of the base year. It is a dynamic method of analysis showing the changes occurred over a period of time. For trend analysis, the study should have at least 5 years' continuous data. This method of analysis exhibits the direction in which a concern is going and basing upon that the future values or forecasting can be estimated.

(ii) Ratio Analysis

Ratio analysis is claimed to be a widely used tool of financial analysis. It is the principal technique used in judging the operational and financial performance of the business enterprise. The analysts, through ratio analysis, can examine not only the performance of the concerned unit but also make a comparison with other units operating in the similar field to find out the strength and weakness of the organization.

The technique of ratio analysis involves four steps viz. selection of appropriate accounting/ financial ratios to be used, computation of the same, comparison of the ratio with the standard one and the interpretation. The last two steps i.e. the comparison and interpretation require careful study and sound judgement on the part of the analysts because there is no clear cut standard for each and every ratio and the interpretation of ratio values is based on careful thought as to the kind of insight the analysts wish to obtain. While studying the financial performance of the OSWC it is felt necessary to study various important ratios falling under the category of liquidity, leverage, activity and profitability.

Apart from financial techniques, statistical techniques such as mean, standard deviation, coefficient of variation and correlation analysis are used to provide a more scientific analysis of the data. Diagrammatic and graphic presentations are made to provide a simplified way of presenting the data for vivid understanding of trends and relationships.

Hypotheses for the Study

1. The Orissa State Warehousing Corporation plays a vital role in the development of the economy of Orissa.

2. The Orissa State Warehousing Corporation plays a leading role in providing storage facilities in Orissa.

3. The income of the Orissa State Warehousing Corporation is mainly dependent upon the own capacity and the occupancy position of its warehouses.

4. The revenues from storage and incidental charges are vital for the survival and growth of the OSWC.

Organisation of the Study

The present study has been organized in seven chapters. The first chapter deals with the importance of the study alongwith the detailed methodology adopted for carrying out the research work. Further the review of literature on the subject has also been included in this chapter. The second chapter presents the origin and growth of warehouses in India and the role of the CWC and the SWCs in the economic development of the country. A brief profile of the OSWC including its objectives, functions, management, area of operation etc. is dealt in the third chapter. The fourth chapter discusses on the physical performance of the OSWC. The fifth chapter deals with the financial performance with regard to the liquidity, solvency and profitability position of the OSWC. The chapter sixth presents the overall picture on manpower utilization in the OSWC. Finally the last chapter includes the summary of the findings of the study along with few suggestions.

Limitation of the Study

The study is based mainly on secondary data collected from the published reports/financial statements of the sample unit and also from different books, journals and periodicals. Therefore, the limitations entailing in the secondary data and financial statements will exist in the study. In spite of limitation, financial statements continue to be a major source of information for micro analysis on firm's behaviour. As the present study deals with a single unit, the inter-firm comparison cannot be made and hence, its actual performance vis-a-vis the other SWCs remain unanswered. The financial techniques such as ratio analysis and trend analysis are used in this study. However, these techniques do have their own limitations. In view of this, the users while utilizing the findings of this study should be careful and judicious in taking decisions.

References

1. G.R. Bhatia, "Agricultural Marketing Research, Surveys and Planning in India" *Agricultural Marketing,* Vol. XXXII, No. 2, July-September, 1989, p. 5.
2. S.K. Mishra and V.K. Puri, *Indian Economy - Its Development Experience,* Himalaya Publishing House, New Delhi, 2001, p. 497.
3. Ruddar Datt and K.P.M. Sundharam, *Indian Economy,* S. Chand and Co. Ltd., New Delhi, 2000, p. 574.
4. Krishna and Gururaj, "Warehousing Corporations : Task Ahead ...", *www.CommodityIndia.com.,* Vol. I, No. 6, August 2001, p. 4.
5. *Ibid.*
6. P.M. Thomas, "Management of Storage, Preservation, Transportation and Processing Foodgrains in India", *Productivity,* Vol. XIV, No. 4, January-March, 1974, pp. 386-401.
7. T.V. Sri. Ram, "Improvement of Storage Conditions and Storage Methods in India", *Productivity,* Vol. XIV, No. 4, January-March, 1974, pp. 402-412.
8. O.N.Chhiber, *Warehousing Corporation in India,* Central Warehousing Corporation, New Delhi, 1982, pp. 229-235.
9. B.R. Choyal, "Pricing in Public Sector : Problems of Pricing in

CWC". *Indian Management* , Vol. 21, No. 12, December, 1982, pp. 19-21.

10. S.C. Sharma, *Warehousing and Distribution- A Study in Agro-Industrial Development*, Uma Publication, New Delhi, 1986, pp. vii-ix.
11. A. Ranganathan, "Warehousing Corporations - A Profile", *Yojana*, Vol.XXX, No. 20, November 1-15, 1986, pp. 22-24.
12. K. S. Gill, D.S. Sidhu and M.S. Sidhu, "Storage Losses of Foodgrains at Firm Level in Punjab", *Agricultural Marketing*, Vol. XXX, No.4, Janurary-March, 1988, pp. 29-33.
13. B. K. Arora and K.V.R. Raju, "Rural Godowns-Where they have failed and How they can Succeed", *Agricultural Marketing*, Vol. XXXIV, No. 1, April-June, 1991, pp. 4-7.

Two

Warehousing Business in India

Introduction

Infrastructure is a vital component for the success of any enterprise, and Warehousing is no exception to this. Warehousing is defined as a scientifically planned infrastructure for orderly accommodation and handling of goods and materials[1]. Warehousing is a trade which involves the deposit of goods, commodities (under the provision of Warehousing Corporations Act, 1962) and wares in the warehouses for safe custody and its return on payment of storage charges. Warehousing is a distinct economic activity. It does not mean preservation of foodgrains alone since it encompasses the facilities and services, incidental or connected with storage, transport, handling and distribution of inputs, products and various other commodities. Warehousing can act as a real and positive contributor to the value of the product[2].

At present, there are three main agencies in the public sector which are engaged in building large-scale storage/ warehousing capacity viz., (i) the Food Corporation of India (FCI), (ii) the Central Warehousing Corporation (CWC) and (iii) 16 State Warehousing Corporations (SWCs).

In India the major players in the field of warehousing business are the CWC and the SWCs. The public sector warehousing was developed in India with the twin objectives of storing agricultural produce and other notified commodities in a scientific manner with pest free condition and preventing the farmers from distress sale of their hard raised crops.

Thus, the role of warehousing is to store the produce of any individual or agency who desires so, on payment of storage charges against the goods stored in the warehouse. Besides commercial activities, the CWC and the SWCs are also engaged themselves in the sphere of Disinfestations Extension Service Scheme, Farmers Extension Service Scheme, imparting training to the in-service personnel, research and development of storage and handling techniques, formulating code of storage practices and also helping the development of warehouses in rural areas.

Since the two public sector enterprises, i.e., the CWC and the SWCs failed to provide adequate storage space, the private bodies have now entered into warehousing business. Initially, it was believed that warehousing business was a capital intensive with low returns and hence the public sector was given the task of developing warehouses in India. However, the notion has changed with the arrival of private enterprises into warehousing business.

Against this backdrop, this chapter aims at discussing the significance of warehousing business, its role in economic development, the emergence of state-run warehousing undertakings etc. in the following pages.

Concept and Meaning of Warehousing

Agriculture is the backbone of the Indian economy. Despite concerted efforts on industrialization during the last five decades, agriculture occupies a place of pride. Being the largest sector in the Indian economy, agriculture provides employment to around 65 per cent of the total work force of the country. Agriculture contributes a major share of national income in India. While comparing the position of agriculture in India with that of other developed countries with regard to the share of agriculture in national income, it is reported that agriculture constituted only 2 per cent of the national income of UK, 3 per cent in USA, 4 per cent in Canada and 5 per cent in Australia[3]. India, having not yet reached the stage of an advanced economy, its agricultural sector is still dominating in the national economy.

Over the years, the agricultural production in the country has increased significantly due to adoption of different patterns of cropping, increase in fertilizer consumption and irrigation facilities and use of improvised seeds. Therefore, need for organized marketing and scientific storage of agricultural and allied products has become inevitable. Further, rural agricultural produce and its storage and distribution remained neglected over the years. In the absence of banking facilities at rural level and lack of purchasing power, the rural farmers had to borrow money on trust from local money lenders at an abnormal high rate of interest. The high rate of interest became an additional cost on the produce and the farmers were left with very negligible return from their investment after paying the loan and interest. In order to intensify the rural activities in the field of agriculture, the arrangement of cheap institutional credit i.e. credit offered by Banking and other institutions was considered a basic necessity. Accordingly, the Co-operative Credit Societies, Land Mortgage Banks and other such institutions were established in rural areas to cater the financial needs of the rural farmers. The Co-operative Banking system used to sanction loans to farmers on the basis of credit worthiness, personal trust and the type of crops grown. The Co-operative Banks arranged advance of loans to its members on the strength of their assets and crop expectation. But the farmers still suffered from keeping the produce with them as they had to sell it after harvest to repay the loan and to meet other requirements. It was, therefore, considered to make the produce itself a good security for raising loans in addition to the general credit worthiness of the farmers. It is in this context that the importance of the concept of 'Warehousing' was duly felt and took a final shape[4].

The term 'Warehouse' consists of two words Ware and House. Ware means articles of trade or manufactured goods meant for sale. House is a common word which requires no explanation. Warehouse may, therefore, be described as building or room or scientific godown constructed for storage of commercial goods meant for sale.

David Foster has defined a 'Warehouse' as "A building into which goods are placed for storage until required for despatch".[5]

Although the terms 'warehouse' and 'warehousing' are interchangeably used but they differ in their meanings. Warehouse refers to a simple protected enclosure or a sophisticated scientific or airconditioned godown. Warehousing is a basic part of the concept of distribution and it covers a package of services, such as, storage, handling, transport, sale, invoicing etc. required in the process of physical distribution system.[6]

Evolution of Warehousing Business

The history with regard to the origin of warehousing still remains in obscurity. However, there exists a strong relationship between the warehousing and agriculture. In order to get an idea of warehouse, it is necessary to understand how agriculture flourished in ancient India.

The study on fossils of paddy seeds discovered in Pratapgarh[7] (Uttar Pradesh) revealed that in ancient India cultivation of paddy was initially started in Allahabad, and then it spreaded over to northwards and westwards. Carbonized paddy grains, grown in between 1000 B.C. and 750 B.C., were uncovered at Hastinapur[8] (Uttar Pradesh). Further, in ancient Indian writings, there are a number of references especially in Atharvaveda dating back to 1500-500 B.C. to the golden grain of wheat.

During the excavation at Mohenjodaro, Harappa and Lothal of Indus Valley Civilization, different types of storage structures were found which were used for storing wheat and rice. These structures belong to a period in between 2500 B.C. and 2000 B.C. and, were made of a mixture of sun-baked and fireclay material.

The available evidences indicate that storage of foodgrains started in Mesolithic period, probably in 8000 B.C., according to Radio Carbon Dating. In the Mesolithic sites at Eynam in North East Israel, many cylindrical storage pits were found in a village in the shape of circular houses. Excavation of Neolithic sites at Fayum near Cairo, capital of Egypt, dating around 4500 B.C., had exposed a large number of small circular grain storage pits with basket work linings or coiled wheat straw. It is presumed that the mouths of these pits were sealed.

In the Old Testament, there is a reference to storage structures. The Egyptian king had not only ordered for the storage of foodgrains during years of bumper harvest but also built enormous structures of large capacities to serve as storage houses for foodgrains.

In Ethiopia, underground storage bins fashioned like bottles were in extensive use. In Bulgaria and Turkey minor caves had served as grain storage godowns. In Tunisia and Greece, dried up wells were used for storage of foodgrains in ancient times. In Venice, warehousing was in vogue. It was called the home of commercial warehousing where warehouse receipts were issued for the goods stored and bankers also accepted them as good security.

The ancient Indian Grammarian Panini, in his great work 'Ashtadhyayi', had referred to many storage vessels like the 6 foot high cylindrical vessel made of earth called 'Kusala', 'Kumbha' with a narrow mouth, 'Kupa' resembling a well, 'Sala' a masonry structure and so on, all with an opening called 'Bila'[9].

'Arthasastra' of Kautilya gives a detailed description of the storage practices followed during the reign of Chandragupta Maurya. Well defined duties of the Keeper of the Crown Storehouses, as they were called, have been mentioned in Arthasastra. The Principal Keeper was called as 'Dhanyadhipa' and the qualification needed to hold that position was that he should be an expert in determining the varieties and grades of the grains as also the techniques to store them in healthy state. The Mauryan rulers had constructed ships with facilities to store huge quantities of foodgrains.

Thus, Indian history provides enough references to foodgrains' store houses during the regime of Cholas, Nayaks and Mahrattas. At Panhala in Maharashtra, there is a large grain storage structure built by Chhattrapatti Shivaji. In Tamil Nadu such type of storage structures are also noticed in the Palace at Thanjavur and another near Tinivaiyur.

With the development of science and technology, different types of storage structures have come into existence in the modern period. Among them are the automatic warehouses which are in operation in the United States of America and Europe. In these warehouses the operations of receipt, storage and delivery are normally carried out mechanically.

Ready to use warehouses are now designed which can move from one place to another as per requirement. Cold storages for storing the perishable goods like fruits, vegetables, dairy and poultry products, and air-conditioned warehouses for storage of drugs and some other perishable goods, have also been set up at different places. Apart from this, the revolution in marketing and international trade has brought about significant changes in the storage practices of different commodities.

The requirement of storage facilities may vary from place to place and from commodity to commodity. Storage facilities are absolutely necessary at the production, assembly and consumption points. These are also required at strategic points to regulate the supply of goods during the period of contingencies. In addition to the technical and locational requirements of storage, other important factors like socio-economic policies are also essential to determine the need for storage management such as necessity of national reserve, buffer stock for local consumption, capacity of warehouses, agency required to manage the warehouses, local practices, availability of materials required for provision of storage facility, climatic conditions and requirements of import and export.

Growth of Warehousing Business in India

The licensed warehouses in India was increasingly felt in the context of the policy of extension of agricultural credit to rural areas. In the same context, it was also felt to provide adequate scientific storage facilities for the preservation of foodgrains and other agricultural produce. The emergence of licensed warehouses in India was the outcome of the implementation of the recommendations made by various Committees constituted to look after the problems faced by the rural mass. A brief discussion on the recommendations of various Committees is being made below.

Royal Commission on Agriculture

The Royal Commission on Agriculture in 1928 recommended the establishment of licensed warehouses.[10] In the year 1944 the Reserve Bank of India issued directives to all the State Governments to enact legislations for the setting up of warehouses in their respective states.

Agricultural Finance Sub-Committee

In the year 1944, the Government of India, in accordance with the recommendations of the Policy Committee on Agriculture, Forestry and Fisheries, appointed a Sub-Committee under the Chairmanship of late Prof. D.R. Gadgil to submit a report suggesting how rural indebtedness could be reduced, and how finance, both short term, and long term, could be provided under efficient control for agriculture and animal husbandry operations.[11] This Committee, in its report submitted in 1945, observed that the volume of finance provided by the commercial banks to the agriculturists could be considerably increased by improving the arrangements for marketing of crops by grading and standardization, creation of proper storage facilities and helping in regulated markets. The Committee felt that the establishment of warehouses in which the goods could be stored through a negotiable receipt useful for obtaining loans from banks should be introduced in India. The Committee was of the view that these steps would open up an important channel for the commercial banks to provide finance to the agriculturists. The Committee also felt that the State should undertake the planning and construction of warehouses at all focal points of trade in agricultural produce and, such a system should be operated by a public corporation.

Rural Banking Enquiry Committee

In the year 1949, the Rural Banking Enquiry Committee was constituted by the Government of India[12]. Among its terms of references the Committee was to consider measures that could be adopted for the extension of banking facilities to the rural areas. In connection with the promotion of warehousing, the committee observed the following.

It has long been recognized that the lack of proper facilities for the storage and warehousing of agricultural produce has been a serious obstacle in the way of increasing the scale of advances against agricultural produce by cooperative marketing societies and commercial banks. Inviting attention to this important impediment, the foreign experts associated with the Central Banking Enquiry Committee remarked, "that considerable improvement of the credit situation and the money market in India can only, under present conditions, be achieved as soon as possible by improving and extending the storage and warehousing of foods in order to enlarge the basis of the credit system"[13].

The Committee recommended that Provincial Governments should consider the desirability of advancing long-term loans at concessional rates of interest to Cooperative Societies to build godowns in such centres which could provide good markets. It also proposed that the Railway Board should also examine the feasibility of either constructing railway warehouses at selected centres or allowing private parties to build such warehouses on favourable terms. The Committee noted that the question of enacting appropriate legislation for licensing warehouses was to be taken up by the Reserve Bank of India and a draft bill on these lines be circulated to the Provincial (or State) Governments. On the model of this bill, Acts were passed in Bombay, Madhya Pradesh, Travancore and Cochin. Inspite of this, no independent warehouse came into existence. The Committee was of the view that without greater initiative and assistance from the State, much progress in this direction was not likely to be achieved.

The Committee further recommended that a Warehousing Development Board be set up with funds contributed by the Central Government, the Reserve Bank of India and the Provincial Governments. In the view of the Committee, this Board was to be charged with the responsibility of promoting warehousing in the country. The Board was to receive, scrutinize and approve applications of commercial banks and cooperative institutions to provide financial assistance for the construction of warehouses in the approved centres with given specifications.

The Committee also recognized the fact that warehousing was a capital intensive activity which might not be attractive to private bodies. Therefore, it advocated that the State should enter into this field. These recommendations, however, did not immediately lead to any tangible result. The construction of adequate scientific storage facilities failed to make much headway despite the efforts and steps taken by the Reserve Bank of India. Little or no interest was shown by the State Governments in the development of public warehousing. These developments, however, underlined the need for the establishment of a central storage agency charged with the responsibility of promoting warehousing in India.

Rural Credit Survey Committee

Public warehousing has originated from the recommendation of the Committee of Direction of the All India Rural Credit Survey Committee. It is, therefore, pertinent to examine the conditions under which the Committee recommended the establishment of Warehousing Corporation in India.[14]

In February 1951, the Reserve Bank of India had convened an informal conference of Co-operators, economists and others including the Registrars of Co-operative Societies of some of the states for considering, among other things, the steps necessary for enlarging the volume of agricultural finance to the agriculturists through the co-operative credit system. This informal conference recommended that the Reserve Bank of India should undertake a rural credit survey which would include all strata of the rural population, and study the problems of capital formation in the rural areas as well as the credit requirement of both the weak and needy farmers. This recommendation was accepted and in August 1951, an All India Rural Credit Survey was constituted under the leadership of Shri B. Rama Rao, the then Governor of the Reserve Bank of India with the following terms of reference :

(i) to direct planning, organization and supervision of the survey;

(ii) to interpret its results; and

(iii) to make recommendations.

The Committee was constituted in the background of the demands reiterated in Parliament that mcre constructive role should be played by the Reserve Bank of India in the sphere of rural credit; and its policies and activities should be reoriented so as to enlarge its participation in the extension of rural credit. The Committee in its reference to the warehousing of the agricultural produce, noted the following findings.

The survey on the problem of rural economy pointed out that lack of adequate and proper storage facilities was an important factor for not getting remunerative price for the agricultural produce. The Committee in its report pinpointed this deficiency and expressed the need for an extensive network of godowns and warehouses and for establishment of licensed warehouses at suitable centres. Emphasis was laid on these aspects by the earlier Committees and Commissions also. The Committee also noted that despite various efforts, the scheme of establishing licensed warehouses had made no progress in any state because most of the existing godowns were not fit to be run as warehouses and, they were only make shift structures, inconveniently situated and were also structurally defective.

The Committee's report on problems of rural economy highlighted the inadequate and improper storage facilities of agricultural produce in rural areas. The inadequacy of the warehousing facilities was the main handicap of the rural farmers as pointed out by the Survey Committee. The Committee, therefore, felt that a concerted effort should be made in this direction to overcome the storage problem in the rural areas.

The concrete recommendations made by the Survey Committee in this regard were:

(1) The establishment of a 'National Board' to be called the 'National Co-operative Development and Warehousing Board' which was to plan and finance the scheme and was to be incharge of the function of storage and warehousing on the one hand, and distribution of basic and standardized requirements of cultivator as a producer and consumer on the other.

(2) The establishment of an All India Corporation with a share capital from the Central Government and various institutions.

(3) The establishment of State Warehousing Corporations in which the State Governments and the All India Corporation were to participate.

(4) The Co-operative Societies were to remain at the base level to cater the needs of farmers. Thus, a multitier-system for the development of scientific storage facilities was conceived by the Committee.

The National Co-operative Development and Warehousing Corporation as well as the Central Warehousing Corporation were to be established by statute; and the State Warehousing Corporations were also to be established by statute.[15]

Based on the recommendations of the All India Rural Credit Survey Committee, the Agricultural Produce (Development and Warehousing) Corporations Act, 1956, was enacted by the Parliament. In this Act, the recommendations made by the aforesaid Committee were broadly incorporated.

Emergence of Public Sector Warehousing

Under the Agricultural Produce (Development and Warehousing) Corporations Act, the Central Warehousing Corporation (CWC) was established. According to the Act, the share capital of the CWC was to be subscribed by National Co-operative (Development and Warehousing) Board and other institutions like the Banks, Co operative Societies, Insurance Companies etc. The shares of the Corporation were guaranteed by the Central Government as to the repayment of the principal and payment of annual dividend at a minimum rate which was to be fixed by the Central Government. The Warehouses of the Corporation could be utilized only for the storage of agricultural and allied produce. There was no provision in the Act to enable the Corporation to take up the storage of commodities other than agricultural produce, inputs and implements.

The Agricultural Produce (Development and Warehousing) Corporations Act also provided for the establishment of State Warehousing Corporations (SWCs) in different States. These Corporations could be established by the State Governments with the approval of the Central Warehousing Corporation. The share capital of the SWC was to be subscribed in equal measure by the Central Warehousing Corporation and the State Government concerned. Thus both the Central Warehousing Corporation and the State Governments were to be equal owners of the State Warehousing Corporations.

Enactment of Warehousing Corporations Act, 1962

In the year 1962, the Agricultural Produce (Development and Warehousing) Corporations Act, 1956 was repealed and was replaced by the Warehousing Corporations Act, 1962.

Under the new Act, the CWC and SWCs, which were already established under the previous Act, were reconstituted. The provisions of the new Act with respect to the Central and State Warehousing Corporations were almost the same with certain changes. The Central Government took-over the place of the National Co-operative (Development and Warehousing) Board in the new Act. Other important changes incorporated in the Act were as follows :

(i) A provision was made in the new Act to enable the Central and State Warehousing Corporations to take up the work of storage of notified commodities (as were notified by the Central Government), agricultural produce, inputs and agricultural implements and their transport to and from the warehouses. This added an important avenue for diversification of the business of the Corporation.

(ii) With regard to the powers of the SWCs to acquire and build godowns at places within the state, a provision was made (Sec. 24) for obtaining the prior approval of the CWC in place of consultation, hitherto provided for, in the previous Act.

(iii) Administration of the Warehousing Fund was transferred from the National Co-operative (Development and Warehousing) Board to the CWC under the new Act. Under the previous Act, the share capital of both the CWC and the SWCs could be subscribed to from this fund. However, under the new Act, the share capital of the CWC neither could be authorised through this Fund nor could the CWC directly contribute to share capital of the SWCs out of this fund.

(iv) Under the previous Act, the SWCs were to subscribe to share capital of Co-operative Societies engaged in storage and warehousing of agricultural produce. This function was eliminated in the new Act.

Thus the basic nature of the relationship between the Central Warehousing Corporation and the State Warehousing Corporations was retained in the new Act. In fact, the control of Central Warehousing Corporation over the State Warehousing Corporations was some what increased. In both the enactments, the organic links, as envisaged by the All India Rural Credit Survey Committee in its report, were recognized.

Evaluation of Performance of the CWC

The Central Warehousing Corporation (CWC) was established in the year 1957 by an Act of Parliament with a view to strengthen the infrastructure for the storage and distribution of the agricultural products. After the creation of the Central

Warehousing Corporation, the era of scientific warehousing in India began. The Corporation was set up with an initial authorised capital of Rs. 20 crores. Over a period of more than four decades, the Central Warehousing Corporation, in addition to its primary activities, diversified its business and achieved multi-dimensional growth. The Central Warehousing Corporation was established on 2nd March, 1957. However, it started functioning in July, 1957 with 7 warehouses having a total capacity of 7000 MT. The CWC now has 451 warehouses all over India with a total capacity of 74.79 lakh MT as on 31st March, 2000.

Objectives and Functions of the CWC

As discussed earlier, both the Agricultural Finance Sub-Committee (1945) and the Rural Banking Enquiry Committee (1950) emphasized the need for warehousing as a method of promoting rural banking and finance in India. An important land mark in the field of warehousing was the recommendation of the All India Rural Credit Survey Committee (1954) for initiating a country-wide programme of warehouse development. This Committee recommended a three-tier system. Under the scheme, warehousing centres of all India importance were to be served by the CWC, centres of secondary markets and district levels were to be served by the SWCs, while the village and the community level warehouses were to be looked after by the Co-operatives.

Objectives

The broad objectives of the Central Warehousing Corporation are:

(i) Creation of negotiable paper to provide an instrument for expansion of credit through Commercial Banks for the benefit of producers, dealers and others;

(ii) Adding to the total nation's real income by reducing waste and losses in storage by promoting and developing warehousing facilities on scientific lines;

(iii) Providing assistance for orderly marketing by introducing standard grade specifications and warehouse receipts;

(iv) Training of personnel to manage and run modern warehouses; and

(v) Providing assistance to Government and Government sponsored Organizations in their scheme of price support and price control.

Functions

The Central Warehousing Corporation performs the following functions as provided in the Warehousing Corporations Act, 1962.

(i) To acquire and build godowns and warehouses at such suitable places in India as it thinks fit.

(ii) To run warehouses for the storage of agricultural produce, seeds, manure, fertilizer, agricultural implements and notified commodities offered by individuals, Co-operative Societies and other Institutions.

(iii) To arrange facilities for the transport of agriculture produce, seeds, manure, fertilizer, agricultural implements and other notified commodities to and from the warehouses.

(iv) To subscribe to the share capital of State Warehousing Corporations.

(v) To act as an agent of the Government for the purpose of purchase, sale, storage and distribution of agricultural produce, seeds, manure, fertilizer, agricultural implements and other notified commodities.

(vi) To carry out such other functions as may be prescribed.

Apart from the above mentioned functions, the CWC also performs some additional functions which are listed below:

(i) The Corporation may act on its own and/or at the request of some parties concerned, to undertake dis-infestation service outside its warehouses in respect of either agricultural produce or the notified commodities.

(ii) The Corporation may at its discretion, act as an agent for the purposes of purchase, sale, storage and distribution of agricultural produce, seeds, manure, fertilizer, agricultural implements and other notified commodities on behalf of a Company (as defined in the Companies Act, 1956, i.e., 1 of 1956), or a body corporate established by the Act of Parliament or of a State legislature or a Co-operative Society.

(iii) It prepares project and renders consultancy service for construction of warehouses at the request of Central Government or any State Government or a Company or a Cooperative Society or to attend to any other matter concerned therewith.

(iv) The Corporation in order to operate warehouses, creates infrastructure and arranges facilities for storage, handling and transport of agricultural produce, seeds, manure, fertilizer, agricultural implements, notified commodities, bonded cargo, air cargo, containerized cargo, liquid cargo etc. It also provides marketing and other warehousing related services in respect of agriculture produce or notified commodities.

(v) The Corporation provides consultancy services, financial assistance etc. related to agricultural produce and other notified commodities, and also undertakes any other activity considered incidental to its functions.

Management of the Central Warehousing Corporation

The management of the Corporation is vested with (i) the Board of Directors, (ii) the Chairman, and (iii) the Managing Director. They form an inter-related and co-ordinated system formulating policies and implementing the same. Though the officers have distinct functions, they work in close collaboration and co-ordination giving unified direction to achieve the goal of the Corporation.

The general superintendence and management of the affairs and business of the Central Warehousing Corporation is vested in the Board of Directors and Executive Committee who with the assistance of the Chairman and Managing Director exercise all the powers and discharge all the functions which may be exercised or discharged by the Central Warehousing Corporation. The Board of Directors act on business principles having regard to public interest and are guided by such instructions on policy matters as may be given to them by the Central Government.

The Board of Directors of the CWC consists of 12 Directors including the Chairman, the Vice-Chairman and the Managing Director. Six Directors are nominated by the Central Government of whom one shall be non-official, and one

Director each is nominated by the National Co-operative Development Corporation (NCDC) and the State Bank of India. There are three elected Directors representing scheduled banks, co-operatives and insurance companies etc. as share holders of the CWC. The term of office of the non-official Director, which is held by the Chairman, is two years from the date of nomination. The term of Directors, nominated by the National Co-operative Development Corporation, State Bank of India and those elected by the respective category of shareholders of the CWC is also for a period of two years from the date of their nomination or election. The term of office of the Managing Director is five years from the date of his appointment. However, an officer of the government or an employee of a government company or a statutory body owned or controlled by the government is also appointed on deputation as Managing Director. The term of office in his case shall be two years (provision for extension exists) from the date of his appointment as Managing Director or till the date of his superannuation, which ever is earlier. The Chairman presides over the meetings of the Board of Directors/Executive Committee. The Board of Directors delegate certain administrative and financial powers to the Chairman. The Managing Director who is the Chief Executive of the Corporation exercises such powers and performs such duties as the Board of Directors may entrust or delegate to him.

Besides the Board of Directors, there is also an Executive Committee of the CWC. The Executive Committee consists of five Directors consisting of the Chairman, the Vice-Chairman and the Managing Director and two Directors are chosen by the other Directors of the Corporation. Of the two Directors one shall be from amongst the elected category of Directors on the Board. The Executive Committee has concurrent powers. However, these are subject to the general control, direction and superintendence of the Board of Directors of the CWC.

Area of Operation of the CWC

The CWC is operating throughout the country having 451 warehouses with a total capacity of 74.79 lakh MT covering 224 districts as on 31.3.2000. The warehouses of the Corporation are used for storage and distribution of foodgrains, fertilizer and other notified commodities. Field units are managed by Warehouse Managers/In-charges. In order to control these field units, 17 Regional Offices are functioning all over the country headed by Regional Managers. The Table 2.1 depicts region-wise capacity of the CWC's warehouses as on 31.3.2000. The table reveals that as against the total capacity of 74.79 lakh MT, the owned capacity is 54.47 lakh MT and hired capacity is 20.32 lakh MT, including 7.88 lakh MT of open and management capacity. A close look into the region-wise capacity further shows that Hyderabad region has the highest capacity of 11.42 lakh MT followed by Lucknow and Mumbai regions with 8.44 lakh MT and 8.02 lakh MT respectively. The lowest capacity of 0.05 lakh MT is marked in Panchkula region. Similarly, the Hyderabad region has the highest constructed capacity of 10.02 lakh MT followed by Lucknow region with 7.66 lakh MT. Like-wise, Chandigarh region has the highest hired capacity of 1.79 lakh MT as on March 31, 2000. The lowest capacity of constructed as well as hired capacity are being marked in Panchkula and Guwahati regions respectively. Apart from normal warehouses, the CWC is also handling containers in 26 Container Freight Station (CFS) at major ports and operating 3 Air Cargo Complexes (ACC) at Amritsar, Goa and Singanallur as on 31.3.2000. By handling cargo through ACCs, the CWC is playing a pivotal role in the growth of international trade.

The customers of the CWC include small farmers, big farmers, co-operatives, traders and business houses, manufactures and industrialists, exporters and importers, government departments and public sector undertakings.

TABLE 2.1

REGION-WISE CAPACITY OF THE CWC AS ON 31.3.2000

(in lakh MT)

Name of the region	*Name of the state*	*Capacity*				
		Constructed	*Hired*	*Open*	*Management*	*Total*
Ahmedabad	Gujarat	2.16	0.53	0.65	0.04	3.38
Bangalore	Karnataka	1.60	0.61	-	0.49	2.70
Bhopal	Madhya Pradesh	5.98	1.41	0.09	0.07	7.50
Bhubaneswar	Orissa	1.36	0.02	0.02	-	1.38
Calcutta	West Bengal	3.22	1.67	0.60	0.01	5.50
Chandigarh	Punjab	4.79	1.79	-	-	6.58
Chandigarh	Chandigarh(UT)	0.11	0.03	0.01	-	0.15
Chennai	Tamil Nadu	5.23	0.57	0.28	-	6.08
Chennai	Pondichery (UT)	0.07	0.03	0.23	-	0.13
Delhi	Delhi	0.98	0.24	0.11	-	1.33
Delhi	Uttar Pradesh	0.73	0.01	-	0.18	0.92
Guwahati	Assam	0.44	0.02	-	0.01	0.47
Guwahati	Mizoram	0.02	-	-	-	0.02
Guwahati	Nagaland	0.13	-	-	-	0.13
Guwahati	Tripura	0.24	-	-	-	0.24
Hyderabad	Andhra Pradesh	10.02	1.05	0.25	0.10	11.42
Jaipur	Rajasthan	1.40	0.52	0.13	0.16	2.21
Kochi	Kerala	0.68	-	-	-	0.68
Lucknow	Uttar Pradesh	7.66	0.60	0.09	0.09	8.44
Mumbai	Goa	0.17	-	-	-	0.17
Mumbai	Maharashtra	3.94	1.62	1.75	0.71	8.02
Navi Mumbai	Maharashtra	0.92	0.27	2.01	-	3.20
Panchkula	Himachal Pradesh	0.05	-	-	-	0.05
Patna	Bihar	1.14	0.36	-	-	1.50
		54.47	**12.44**	**5.99**	**1.89**	**74.79**

Source: Compiled from the Annual Report of the CWC, New Delhi, 1999-2000.

The warehouses of the CWC provide storage facilities and ancillary services to more than 250 types of commodities and products. Table 2.2 shows the commodity-wise utilization of storage capacity during the years from 1995-96 to 1999-2000. The table reveals that foodgrains and fertilizer taken together handled more than 50 per cent of the storage space during the period under study as compared to other commodities. The report of the Corporation reveals that the CWC has handled 25.78 lakh MT of foodgrains, 7.86 lakh MT of fertilizer and 23.16 lakh MT of other commodities during 1999-2000.[16]

Storage Capacity and Its Utilization

The warehousing capacity of the CWC has grown over the years. The details of growth in storage capacity and its utilization have been depicted in Table 2.3. It is observed from the table that over a period of five years i.e. from 1995-96 to 1999-2000, the CWC has added additional 3.17 lakh MT of its own constructed godowns to its existing capacity and likewise, it has added the hired capacity by another 1.87 lakh MT. Thus the total capacity of both own and hired increased to 5.04 lakh MT.

TABLE 2.2

COMMODITY-WISE UTILIZATION OF STORAGE CAPACITY OF THE CWC

(in %)

Year	*Foodgrains*	*Fertilizer*	*Others*	*Total*
1995-96	41	15	44	100
1996-97	38	13	49	100
1997-98	44	14	42	100
1998-99	41	15	44	100
1999-2000	41	15	44	100

Source: Compiled from the Annual Reports of the CWC, New Delhi.

TABLE 2.3
YEAR-WISE DISTRIBUTION OF STORAGE CAPACITY AND UTILIZATION OF THE CWC

(in lakh MT)

Year	Owned	Hired	Total	Average occupancy	% of utilization
1995-96	51.30	18.45	69.75	56.57	81.81
1996-97	51.93	19.26	71.19	51.26	72.00
1997-98	52.29	19.99	72.28	52.16	72.16
1998-99	53.65	19.83	73.48	53.74	72.77
1999-2000	54.47	20.32	74.79	56.84	75.94

Source: Compiled from the Annual Reports of the CWC, New Delhi, 1995-2000 and, Annual Report of Ministry of Consumer Affairs, Food and Public Distribution, Department of Food and Public Distribution, New Delhi., 2000-2001.

Further the capacity utilization of the Central Warehousing Corporation for the period from 1995-96 to 1999-2000 has been given in the table. The table exhibits that the percentage of occupancy showed a fluctuating trend and hovered between 72 per cent and 81 per cent. Though, there was an increase in the capacity during the study period, yet a corresponding increase was not marked in the capacity utilization.

From the foregoing analysis it can be concluded that the CWC as a premier organization in providing storage facilities for agricultural produce and allied items has spread its net work all over the country. The CWC has vast storage facilities in certain regions like Hyderabad, Lucknow, Mumbai etc. So far as its storage facilities utilization is concerned, foodgrain has taken the lead followed by fertiliser. It is observed that in none of the years of the study period the Corporation has utilized fully its capacity which is a matter of concern and needs urgent attention.

Financial Performance of the CWC

The CWC has been making profit in-spite of highly competitive environment. The income, expenditure and profit figures of the CWC for the period from 1995-96 to 1999-2000 is depicted in Table 2.4. While the table exhibits a rising trend for both the income and expenditure, the profit figure reveals fluctuating trend. The net profit during the period was ranging from Rs. 41.50 crores to Rs. 84.95 crores.

TABLE 2.4
INCOME AND EXPENDITURE POSITION OF THE CWC

(Rs. in Crores)

Year	*Income*	*Expenditure*	*Profit*
1995-96	209.30	148.32	60.98
1996-97	234.68	149.73	84.95
1997-98	253.34	185.61	67.73
1998-99	255.64	214.14	41.50
1999-2000	276.34	228.04	48.30

Source: Compiled from the Annual Reports of the CWC, New Delhi.

The main source of revenue of the CWC is warehousing charges. The other sources of income are from agency commission on incidental services provided to the depositors, dividend received on investment made on the State Warehousing Corporations, interest earned on short and long term deposits as also receipts from other sources. The items of expenditure of the CWC include establishment, rent, insurance, disinfestations, dunnage, depreciation on equipments and other contingencies.

Promotional Activities

In the stupendous task of building the food reserves of our nation and organizing orderly supply of foodgrains, the CWC has been making a positive promotional contribution through its warehousing infrastructure and connected services. The CWC takes care of the need for disinfestations of commodities stored outside its warehouses through its "Disinfestation Extension Service Scheme" (DESS). It also disseminates knowledge and information concerning scientific storage techniques to the farming community under its "Farmers Extension Service Scheme" (FESS).

Disinfestation Extension Service Scheme (DESS)

The DESS was launched by the CWC in 1966 with a view to extend the advantage of scientific storage and preservation at the door steps of the customers including farmers. Under this scheme, the pest control services are provided to the farmers and traders to control the damages caused by insects and rodents. Apart from this, the fumigation of exportable foodgrains is also undertaken from time to time. In addition to these, disinfestations of aircrafts, railway coaches, various office building premises and hotels etc. are also undertaken to generate additional revenue. During the period from 1995-96 to 1999-2000 the CWC generated Rs. 787.33 lakhs under the DES Scheme.[17]

Farmers Extension Service Scheme (FESS)

As a promotional activity, the FESS was launched by the CWC during the year 1978-79 with the following objectives.

(a) To educate farmers about the benefit of scientific storage and use of public warehouses.

(b) To impart training to the farmers on the techniques of scientific storage and preservation of foodgrains.

(c) Demonstration of spraying and fumigation method to control insects.

(d) To assist farmers in getting loan from the Banks against pledge of warehouse receipts.

Keeping these points in view the scheme is being operated through 205 warehouses all over the country. During the last five years 7,56,623 farmers have been educated on methods of scientific preservation/post-harvest technology.[18]

It can be mentioned here that apart from the storage, handling and distribution of agricultural produce and allied items, the CWC also discharges certain promotional activities like FESS and DESS thereby contributing significantly to the national economy.

Evaluation of Performance of the SWCs

The State Warehousing Corporations Act, 1962, provides that "a State Government may, by notification in the Official Gazette and with the approval of Central Warehousing Corporation establish a Warehousing Corporation for the State under such name as may be specified in the notification". As per the provisions of the Act, 16 states in India have established their respective Warehousing Corporations mostly during late fifties. The initial capital of the SWCs were equally contributed by the CWC and the concerned State Government.

Objectives and Functions of the SWCs.

The objective, scope, function and management of State Warehousing Corporations are more or less same as prescribed to the Central Warehousing Corporation. However, the area of operation of a State Warehousing Corporation is confined within the state concerned. The functions of the State Warehousing Corporation as defined under Section 24 of Warehousing Corporations Act, 1962, are as follows :

(i) To acquire and build godowns and warehouses at such places within the state as it may desire, with the previous approval of the CWC;

(ii) To run warehouses in the state for storage of agricultural produce, seeds, manure, fertilizer, agricultural implements and other notified commodities;

(iii) To arrange facilities for transportation of agricultural produce, seeds, manure, fertilizer, agricultural implements and other notified commodities to and from the warehouses;

(iv) To act as an agent of the CWC or the Government for purchase, sale, storage and distribution of agricultural produce, seeds, manure, fertilizer, agricultural implements and notified commodities; and

(v) To carry out such other functions as may be prescribed.

A few State Warehousing Corporations are also performing additional functions which are being performed by the Central Warehousing Corporation.

Management of State Warehousing Corporations

The general superintendence and management of the affairs of a State Warehousing Corporation is vested in a Board of Directors which consist of 10 Directors. A Managing Director is appointed by the concerned State Government in consultation with the Directors and with the previous approval of the CWC. Further, the Chairman of the Board of Directors shall be appointed by the concerned State Government from among the Directors of the SWC with the previous approval of the CWC. The Managing Director exercises such powers and performs such duties as the Board of Directors or the SWC may entrust or delegate to him.

The Board of Directors shall act on business principles having regard to public interest and shall be guided by such instructions on questions of policy as may be given to them by State Government or the CWC.

Besides, there is an Executive Committee of a State Warehousing Corporation consisting the Chairman, the Managing Director and three other Directors. The Chairman of the Board of Directors shall be Chairman of the Executive Committee. The Board of Directors and the Executive Committee have been entrusted to manage the Corporation.

At present sixteen State Warehousing Corporations are operating throughout the Country. The name and year of the establishment of State Warehousing Corporations have been given in Table 2.5.

TABLE 2.5

YEAR-WISE ESTABLISHMENT OF THE SWCS

Sl. No.	*Name of the SWCs*	*Date of establishment*
1.	Bihar SWC	29.03.1957
2.	Maharastra SWC	08.08.1957
3.	Karnataka SWC	08.08.1957
4.	Rajasthan SWC	02.12.1957
5.	Tamil Nadu SWC	04.12.1957
6.	Punjab SWC	02.01.1958
7.	Madhya Pradesh SWC	29.02.1958
8.	Uttar Pradesh SWC	19.03.1958
9.	Orissa SWC	21.03.1958
10.	West Bengal SWC	01.06.1958
11.	Andhra Pradesh SWC	05.08.1958
12.	Assam SWC	12.08.1958
13.	Kerala SWC	20.02.1959
14.	Gujarat SWC	05.12.1959
15.	Haryana SWC	01.11.1967
16.	Meghalaya SWC	30.03.1973

Source: O.N. Chhiber, Warehousing Corporations in India, New Delhi, 1982, p.180.

The table reveals that most of State Warehousing Corporations were established in between 1957 and 1958. The first SWC was established in the state of Bihar on 29.3.1957 and the last SWC was established in the state of Meghalaya on 30.3.1973.

Storage Capacity of the SWCs

The position of storage capacity alongwith the number of warehouse godowns of 16 State Warehousing Corporations as on 31.3.2000 are indicated in Table 2.6. It is seen from the table that Punjab State Warehousing Corporation has got the highest capacity with 30.58 lakh MT as on March 2000. It is followed by Uttar Pradesh with 17.61 lakh MT and Madhya Pradesh with 16.83 lakh MT as on the same date. It is further noticed that in most of the states, the owned capacity of the SWCs is more than the hired capacity except the Bihar SWC. However, in states like Karnataka, Punjab and West Bengal the owned and hired capacity of the warehouses are more or less evenly distributed. From the above figures, one thing is clear that the SWCs give importance to construct their own godowns for better supervision and maintenance of the stock.

Capacity Utilization

The capacity utilization of the SWCs is presented in Table 2.7. It is seen from the table that on the whole 84.50 per cent of the total capacity was utilized by the SWCs as on 31st March, 2000. On individual basis the states namely, Karnataka, Meghalaya and Uttar Pradesh have utilized more than the total capacity available with them. On the contrary, the capacity utilization of warehouses of Kerala, Rajasthan, Haryana and West Bengal was unsatisfactory because nearly one-third of the total capacity remained unutilized as on the said date. The utilization of capacity in case of rest SWCs ranged in between 74 per cent and 96 per cent. From the above analysis, it is clear that the capacity utilization of eight SWCs remained below the national average which is 84.50 per cent during 1999-2000.

TABLE 2.6
CAPACITY OF WAREHOUSES OF THE SWCS AS ON 31ST MARCH, 2000

(in lakh MT)

Name of the SWCs	*No. of warehouses*	*Capacity*			*Total*
		Owned	*Hired*	*Plinth*	
Andhra Pradesh	69	4.14	2.90	-	7.04
Assam	41	1.82	0.74	0.02	2.58
Bihar	46	1.09	1.65	-	2.74
Gujarat	48	1.35	0.09	-	1.44
Haryana	104	6.12	2.19	2.18	10.49
Karnataka	107	2.88	2.56	-	5.44
Kerala	61	1.60	0.33	-	1.93
Madhya Pradesh	324	12.77	4.05	0.01	16.83
Maharashtra	150	8.67	0.88	-	9.55
Meghalaya	5	0.11	-	-	0.11
Orissa	63	1.64	0.82	-	2.46
Punjab	107	15.09	14.15	1.34	30.58
Rajasthan	83	5.63	0.50	-	6.13
Tamil Nadu	65	5.98	0.29	-	6.27
Uttar Pradesh	132	11.94	5.67	-	17.61
West Bengal	32	1.37	1.17	-	2.54
Total	**1440**	**82.20**	**37.99**	**3.55**	**123.74**

Source: Compiled from the Annual Reports and Records of the SWCs.

TABLE 2.7
CAPACITY UTILIZATION OF SWCS AS ON 31ST MARCH, 2000

(in lakh MT)

Name of the SWCs	*No. of centres*	*Total capacity*	*Average occupancy*	*Percentage of occupancy*
Andhra Pradesh	69	7.04	6.73	95.59
Assam	41	2.58	2.02	78.29
Bihar	46	2.74	2.36	86.13
Gujarat	48	1.44	1.07	74.30
Haryana	104	10.49	7.20	68.63
Karnataka	107	5.44	5.51	101.28
Kerala	61	1.93	1.32	68.39
Madhya Pradesh	324	16.83	12.93	76.82
Maharashtra	150	9.55	9.16	95.91
Meghalaya	5	0.11	0.12	109.09
Orissa	63	2.46	2.20	89.43
Punjab	107	30.58	24.39	79.75
Rajasthan	83	6.13	4.03	65.74
Tamil Nadu	65	6.27	6.00	95.69
Uttar Pradesh	132	17.61	17.81	101.13
West Bengal	32	2.54	1.71	67.32
Total	**1440**	**123.74**	**104.56**	**84.50**

Source: Compiled from the Annual Reports and Records of the SWCs.

Area of Operation

In order to boost the warehousing activities, many states have established their own Warehousing Corporation. The area of operation of the SWC is limited to the state itself as defined in the Warehousing Corporations Act, 1962. Like the CWC, the chief commodities accepted for storage in the warehouses of the SWCs are foodgrains, fertilizer, oil seeds, pulses and other notified commodities. The Table 2.8 visualises the commodity-wise utilization of space by the SWCs. The said table also reveals that the Haryana, Uttar Pradesh and Orissa SWCs accommodated more foodgrains stock ranging from 65 per cent to 83 per cent than other commodities. Similarly, the Bihar SWC and West Bengal SWC accepted more fertilizer stock than foodgrains stock ranging in between 58 per cent and 82 per cent. The Gujarat SWC and Madhya Pradesh SWC accommodated more notified commodities like cotton bales, Kendu leaves and industrial goods.

TABLE 2.8

COMMODITY-WISE UTILIZATION OF SPACE BY THE SWCS AS ON 31.3.2000

(in %)

Name of the SWCs	*Commodity-wise utilization*			*Total*
	Foodgrains	*Fertilizer*	*Others **	
Andhra Pradesh	56	26	18	100
Assam	NA	NA	NA	NA
Bihar	12	82	6	100
Gujarat	14	20	66	100
Haryana	83	15	2	100
Karnataka	60	33	7	100
Kerala	NA	NA	NA	NA
Madhya Pradesh	35	10	55	100
Maharashtra	29	23	48	100
Meghalaya	NA	NA	NA	NA
Orissa	65	32	3	100
Punjab	NA	NA	NA	NA
Rajasthan	38	38	26	100
Tamil Nadu	NA	NA	NA	NA
Uttar Pradesh	76	12	12	100
West Bengal	8	58	34	100

* Others include Notified Commodities

NA: Not Available.

Source: Compiled from the Annual Reports and Records of the SWCs.

The major customers of the SWCs are Government Departments, Public Sector Undertakings, Exporters, Importers, Industrial houses, Traders, Co-operative Organisations, small and marginal farmers etc. However, it is observed from the report that the major depositors of the SWCs are the Public Sector Organisations.

Financial Performance of the SWCs

The financial performance i.e. the net income/loss generated by the SWCs is presented in Table 2.9. The table depicts that except the Gujarat SWC all other SWCs have generated profit during 1999-2000. The states namely Haryana, Maharashtra, Punjab and Uttar Pradesh have generated huge profit. On the other hand, the states namely, Assam, Kerala and Meghalaya earned marginal profit. A close look into the Table further envisages that the profit margin of many SWCs is low due to huge expenditure incurred by them.

From the overall analysis of physical and financial performance of the SWCs, it is marked that the states namely, Uttar Pradesh, Meghalaya and Karnataka have utilized beyond the full capacity. Further the SWCs of Haryana and Uttar Pradesh have handled more foodgrain stocks than other SWCs. On the contrary, the West Bengal SWC and Bihar SWC have accorded top priority for storing fertilizer. From the financial performance point of view, the SWCs of Punjab, Haryana, Maharashtra and Uttar Pradesh have generated huge profit during 1999-2000. The analysis further reveals that the physical and financial performance of Orissa State Warehousing Corporation is moderate when compared to the average performance of all the SWCs taken together.

TABLE 2.9
INCOME AND EXPENDITURE POSITION OF THE SWCS AS ON 31ST MARCH, 2000

(Rs. in Crores)

Name of the SWCs	*Income*	*Expenditure*	*Profit*	*Loss*
Andhra Pradesh	13.77	8.68	5.09	-
Assam	5.51	5.50	0.01	-
Bihar	13.71	11.41	2.30	-
Gujarat	3.06	3.54	-	0.47
Haryana	29.77	16.72	16.72	-
Karnataka	13.51	9.17	4.33	-
Kerala	8.65	8.46	0.19	-
Madhya Pradesh	35.88	31.38	4.49	-
Maharashtra	54.66	38.56	16.10	-
Meghalaya	0.27	0.19	0.05	-
Orissa	13.47	12.25	1.21	-
Punjab	68.12	46.10	22.01	-
Rajasthan	17.15	10.24	6.91	-
Tamil Nadu	13.84	10.29	3.54	-
Uttar Pradesh	99.59	83.02	16.56	-
West Bengal	9.75	7.22	2.52	-
Total	**400.71**	**302.75**	**98.38**	**0.47**

Source. Compiled from the Annual Reports and Records of the SWCs.

Role of Warehousing in Economic Development

Storage of goods is of vital importance not only in the agriculture sector but also in the industrial sector. In the primary sector, i.e., agriculture, storage is necessary at the farm and field level; in the secondary sector, i.e., industry, storage is essential at the processing and manufacturing level; and in the tertiary sector, it is inevitable for the domestic, import and export trade[19].

One of the prerequisites for the economic development of a country is the growth of storage facilities. The necessity for storage arises primarily because of lack of adjustment between the time and place of production of goods, and time and place of their consumption. Further, the need for storage also arises from the division of labour.

Any programme or project on agricultural and industrial development should have a component of proper and adequate storage facilities. If this important aspect of physical distribution is ignored at the initial stage of planning then it will have adverse affect on subsequent stages of production and distribution. Therefore, it is recognised that warehousing facilities, in all the sectors of the economy, need careful planning.

In the changing scenario, the pattern of production, intra and inter-state trading activities, mode of transportation and the systems of marketing have brought different types of warehouses to suit the requirements of trade. In the trade and commerce, there is the necessity of warehousing services. Warehouses provide flexibility and versatility in the movement of goods. It also economises space, labour cost, and distribution cost.

Warehousing plays a vital role in the flow of goods from producer to consumer. It helps in combating annual and seasonal fluctuation in production and prices. The self-sufficient economy has been replaced by the "money and exchange economy" through evolutionary processes. The economic growth of a nation is influenced by its socio-economic conditions, political set-up, climatic condition, geography, religion, habits and habitants of general masses. The agricultural produce or goods are partly utilized by the producers themselves and partly disposed of to consumers.

The later portion of the produce is called "marketable surplus" which gives birth to the creation of storage infrastructures for storing of produce/goods. Like-wise during the period of scarcity of foodgrains and emergency situations the need of warehousing is felt. Thus Warehousing serves the functions of a reservoir which has a great role in the economic development of a country.[20]

Prospects and Challenges of Warehousing Business during the Liberalization Era

Even though Warehousing business in India has a bright future, still it has to face a number of challenges from many corners. The Warehousing business is directly dependent on the vagaries of weather, production of foodgrains and fertilizer, import of fertilizer and availability of industrial raw materials, finished products and other notified commodities. Moreover, buffer stock is one of the contributing factors for maximum utilization of storage space. Since warehousing is a capital intensive business, only public sector was encouraged to conduct warehousing business. However, with the formulation and announcement of National Storage Policy by Government of India, the Warehousing business is going to pave the way for the private sectors. The major feature of National Storage Policy is that government has given it the status of infrastructure. According to the policy, many incentives and assistance will be made available to this sector. Once private participation in the field of warehousing is allowed, the so-called monopoly of Warehousing business by the public sectors will disappear and hence affect their business prospect. Now it is considered as the greatest challenge before the Public Sector Warehousing Undertakings in the post liberalization era. However, the quality of service, the price, etc. will decide their survival in the ensuing competitive environment.

India has made considerable progress in all fronts. Further the post liberalization era has brought a sea change in the Indian economy. If the agricultural and industrial sectors grow as projected by the planners, there will be heavy demand for storage facilities in the coming years. The population of India is now over 100 crores and given the present growth rate in population, India will be the most populated country in the world in future. Accordingly, the planners and the policy makers are trying to increase the foodgrains production through improved methods of cultivation. Further, the demand for fertilizer, pesticides etc. will go up. Hence, the demand for warehouses to accommodate them will be more in the future. Apart from foodgrains production, various kinds of durable and non-durable goods will register further increase. Besides maintaining buffer stock of foodgrains, the Government has to keep buffer stock of fertilizer, sugar and other essential commodities including raw materials required for industries. All these factors are contributing to the prospect of Warehousing business in India. In order to make this system effective and complete, there is a need for a well designed network of strategically located public warehouses in the country. The public warehouses will definitely form an integral part of any future programme on production and distribution of agricultural and industrial commodities. Therefore, the expansion of public warehouses, as also the warehousing business, seems to go a long way in developing the Indian economy in the years to come.

References

1. S.C. Sharma, *Warehousing and Distribution- A Study in Agro-Industrial Development*, Uma Publication, New Delhi, 1986, p. 1.
2. *Ibid.*, p. 26.
3. Ruddar Datt and K.P.M Sundharam, *Indian Economy*, Sultan Chand and Co., New Delhi, 2000, p. 447.
4. *Manual of the Central Warehousing Corporation*, Vol. I, 1982, p. 1.

5. S.C. Sharma, *op. cit.*, p. 25.
6. *Ibid.*, p. 26.
7. O.N. Chhiber, *Warehousing Corporations in India.*, New Delhi, 1982, p. 1.
8. *Ibid.*
9. *Ibid.*, p. 2.
10. S. C. Sharma, *op. cit.*, p. 15.
11. *Ibid.*
12. O.N. Chhiber, *op.cit.*, pp. 4-5.
13. *Ibid.*, p. 4ff.
14. *Ibid.*, p. 6.
15. S.C. Sharma, *op. cit.* p. 19.
16. Annual Report, Central Warehousing Corporation, New Delhi, 1999-2000, p. 4.
17. *Ibid.*, p. 115.
18. *Ibid.*, p. 15.
19. O. N. Chhiber, *op. cit.*, p. 31.
20. *Ibid*, pp. 31-32.

Three

A Brief Profile of the Orissa State Warehousing Corporation

Introduction

The Orissa State Warehousing Corporation (OSWC) was established in 1958 with the objectives of providing an instrument for easy institutional credit to the needy farmers and to minimize storage losses of foodgrains and other agricultural produce. In the initial period, the Corporation had only two hired godowns with a total capacity of 860 MT. However, the number of warehouses had gone up to 63 with a total capacity of 2,46,660 MT spreading over in 27 districts as on March, 2000. Over the years it has made a modest progress to achieve its objectives as laid down in Warehousing Corporations Act, 1962. Moreover, the Corporation is engaging itself in construction of warehouses to provide infrastructural facilities for scientific storage and distribution of commodities in the remote areas of the state.

Agriculture is the backbone of the state's economy. The economy of Orissa is mainly dependent on agriculture and allied activities. The efforts of the State Government are always directed towards the betterment of the economic conditions of the farmers, particularly small and marginal farmers, by providing them with improved varieties of seeds, fertilizer and other facilities at their door steps to increase production. It is in this background, the role of the OSWC assumes significance in meeting the requirement of safe and scientific storage of the agriculture and allied produce.

The implementation of scientific techniques in cultivation, use of high yielding seeds, fertilizer and expansion of irrigation facilities through major irrigation projects, the production of foodgrains in the state touched a new height. The OSWC is building storage facilities to accommodate the growing agricultural produce of the state. Besides, the use of chemicals, fertilizer and pesticides in the state is growing steadily. Though the use of these inputs is seasonal, yet there is a need to provide them warehousing facilities throughout the year to avoid the shortage at the time of requirement. Warehousing of fertilizer and pesticides is necessary to achieve self- sufficiency in foodgrains for the greater interest of the nation, and the state in particular. Thus, Warehousing system provides safe storage of agricultural produce and other notified commodities in a scientific manner. Any depositor can store the commodities by paying a nominal storage charge fixed by the Corporation from time to time. The Warehousing Corporation gives a receipt to the depositor stating the quantity, quality of goods and the delivery date of the deposit. The Corporation provides protection of the stocks against fire, burglary, theft, floods, cyclone etc. In other words, it ensures safe return of goods to the depositor on the due date. That apart, the banking institution accepts the warehouse receipts given by the Corporation as a good security and advances loans to the holder of the receipt. Therefore, the need for warehousing has become more prominent in recent years and its importance is growing day by day.

Origin of the Orissa State Warehousing Corporation

The Agricultural Produce (Development and Warehousing) Corporations Act, 1956 was enacted by the Parliament which came into force on 1.8.1956. The Orissa State Legislature enacted the Orissa Warehouse Act, 1956 (Orissa Act 4 of 1957) to encourage the establishment of Licensed

Warehouses and make provision for their control and supervision. The OSWC was set up by the State Government complying with the provision of 28(1) of Act 28 of 1956 by Notification dated 21.3.1958.[1]

Objectives of the OSWC

The OSWC was established keeping in view the following objectives.

(i) Stabilisation of price of agricultural produce and expansion of institutional credit to agriculture through warehouse receipts.

(ii) Preventing post-harvest storage losses by constructing modern and scientific godowns.

(iii) Assisting the Government in storage and distribution of essential commodities to ensure price control.

(iv) Storing the agricultural inputs like fertilizer, pesticides and seeds with a view to remove the bottlenecks in distribution.

(v) Storing other commodities which are vital for the development of industry and trade.

Functions of the OSWC

The OSWC performs a number of activities. However, the important functions of the Corporation are as follows:

(i) To acquire and build godowns and warehouses at such places within the state, as it may be necessary with the prior approval of the Central Warehousing Corporation.

(ii) To run warehouses in the state for the storage of agricultural produce, seeds, manure, fertilizer, agricultural implements and notified commodities.

(iii) To arrange facilities for the transport of agricultural produce, seeds etc. to and from warehouses.

(iv) To act as an agent of either the Central Warehousing Corporation or the Government for the purpose of the purchase, sale, storage and distribution of agricultural produce, seeds, manure, fertilizer etc.

(v) Last but not the least, to carry out such other functions as may be directed from time to time.

Management of the OSWC

The general superintendence and management of the affairs of the State Warehousing Corporation is vested in a Board consisting of 10 Directors which are in the following manner.

(a) five directors nominated by the Central Warehousing Corporation of whom one shall be nominated in consultation with the State Bank of India and another one at least be a non-official.

(b) five directors nominated by the State Government and

(c) a Managing Director, appointed by the State Government in consultation with the directors referred to in clause (a) and (b) of Warehousing Corporations Act, 1962 and with the previous approval of the Central Warehousing Corporation. However, as per the Warehousing Corporations

(Amendment) Act, 2001, the word "Previous approval of" has been substituted to "under intimation to". Further, the Chairman of the Board of Directors shall be appointed by the State Government from among the directors of the OSWC under intimation to the Central Warehousing Corporation. The Managing Director exercises such powers and performs such duties as the Board of Directors or the State Warehousing Corporation may entrust or delegate to him.

The Board of Directors shall act on business principles having regard to public interest and shall be guided by such instructions on questions of policy as may be given to them by the State Government or the Central Warehousing Corporation. In case any doubt arises on the matter of policy, e.g., if the State Government and the Central Warehousing Corporation give conflicting instructions, the matter shall be referred to the Central Government whose decision there on shall be final.

Apart from this, there is an Executive Committee of the State Warehousing Corporation which shall consist of :

(i) The Chairman of the Board of Directors;

(ii) The Managing Director; and

(iii) Three other directors chosen in the prescribed manner of whom one shall be a Director referred to in clause (a) of sub-section (1) of Section 20 of the Warehousing Corporations Act, 1962.

The Chairman of the Board of Directors shall be Chairman of the Executive Committee. The Board of Directors and the Executive Committee have been entrusted to manage the Corporation.

In a nutshell, the top management of the Corporation vests in (i) the Board of Directors, (ii) the Chairman, and (iii) the Managing Director.

They form an inter-related and coordinated system for formulating policy and implementing it. Though the officers have distinct functions, they work in close collaboration and co-ordination giving unified direction to the Corporation. The management structure of the OSWC is presented in Fig. 3.1.

Financial Structure

The share capital of the OSWC at the time of its inception was only Rs. 10 lakh contributed on 50:50 basis both by the Central Warehousing Corporation and the Orissa State Government. Thereafter, the share capital of the Corporation had increased from time to time and at present the share capital stands at Rs. 360 lakh. As against a total capital of Rs. 360 lakh the total assets of the Corporation is Rs. 2697.91 lakh. The net-worth position of the OSWC is Rs. 920.40 lakh as on 31.3.2000. Like-wise the long term debt position is Rs. 33.51 lakh as on March 31, 1999. However, during 1999-2000 the OSWC has no long term loans in its capital structure.

Area of Operation of the OSWC

The total geographical area of the state comprising 30 districts is 1,55,707 square kilometers[2] as reported by the Surveyor General of India. The OSWC is functioning in 27 districts out of 30 districts of the state for storage and distribution of foodgrains, fertilizer and other notified commodities. Field units are managed by Warehouse Superintendents/ In-charges. To control the field units 10 zones have been created. The zone-wise distribution of warehouses as on 31.3.2000 is presented in Table 3.1.

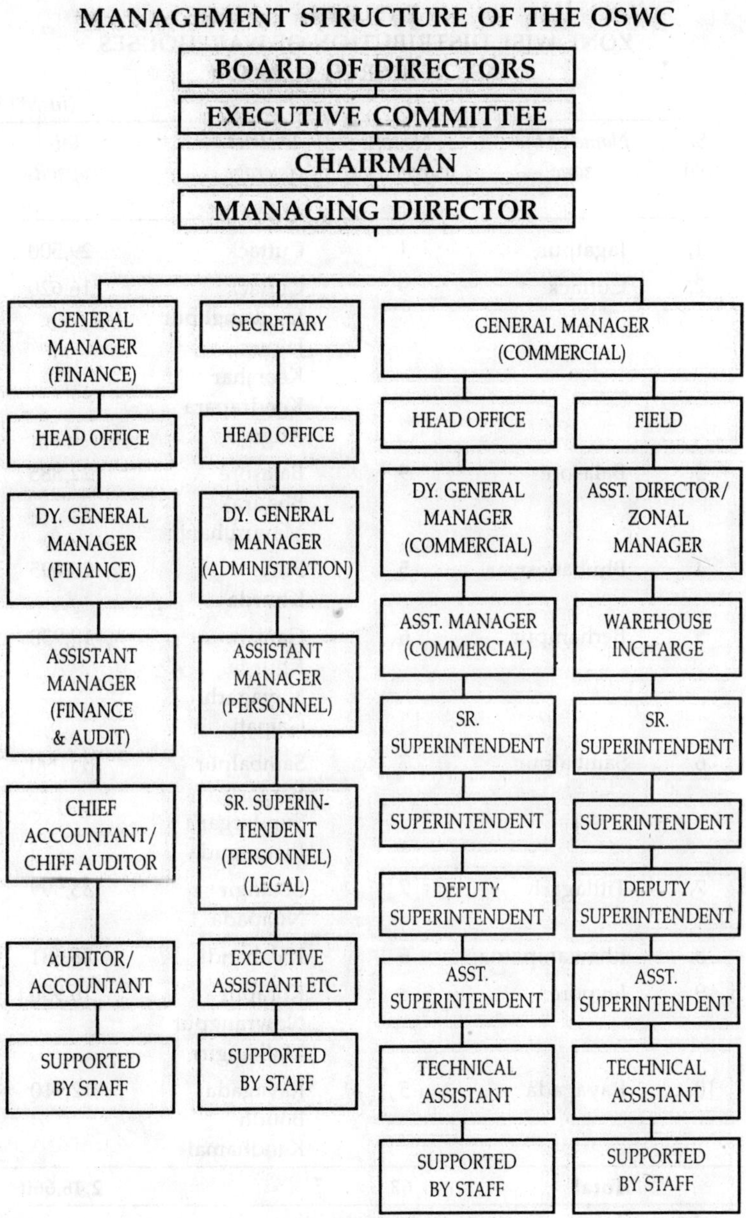
MANAGEMENT STRUCTURE OF THE OSWC
BOARD OF DIRECTORS
EXECUTIVE COMMITTEE
CHAIRMAN
MANAGING DIRECTOR
GENERAL MANAGER (FINANCE)
HEAD OFFICE
DY. GENERAL MANAGER (FINANCE)
ASSISTANT MANAGER (FINANCE & AUDIT)
CHIEF ACCOUNTANT/ CHIFF AUDITOR
AUDITOR/ ACCOUNTANT
SUPPORTED BY STAFF
SECRETARY
HEAD OFFICE
DY. GENERAL MANAGER (ADMINISTRATION)
ASSISTANT MANAGER (PERSONNEL)
SR. SUPERIN-TENDENT (PERSONNEL) (LEGAL)
EXECUTIVE ASSISTANT ETC.
SUPPORTED BY STAFF
GENERAL MANAGER (COMMERCIAL)
HEAD OFFICE
DY. GENERAL MANAGER (COMMERCIAL)
ASST. MANAGER (COMMERCIAL)
SR. SUPERINTENDENT
SUPERINTENDENT
DEPUTY SUPERINTENDENT
ASST. SUPERINTENDENT
TECHNICAL ASSISTANT
SUPPORTED BY STAFF
FIELD
ASST. DIRECTOR/ ZONAL MANAGER
WAREHOUSE INCHARGE
SR. SUPERINTENDENT
SUPERINTENDENT
DEPUTY SUPERINTENDENT
ASST. SUPERINTENDENT
TECHNICAL ASSISTANT
SUPPORTED BY STAFF

Fig. 3.1

TABLE 3.1
ZONE-WISE DISTRIBUTION OF WAREHOUSES AS ON MARCH 31, 2000.

(in MT)

Sl. No.	*Name of the zone*	*No. of warehouses*	*District coverage*	*Total capacity*
1.	Jagatpur	1	Cuttack	29,500
2.	Cuttack	9	Cuttack Jagatsinghpur Jajpur Keonjhar Kendrapara Angul	16,620
3.	Balasore	9	Balasore Bhadrak Mayurbhanj	22,885
4.	Bhubaneswar	5	Puri Khurda	28,495
5.	Berhampur	6	Ganjam Khurda Nayagarh Gajpati	19,930
6.	Sambalpur	7	Sambalpur Bargarh Sundargarh Jharsuguda	35,090
7.	Titilagarh	7	Bolangir Nuapada	35,599
8.	Bhawanipatna	6	Kalahandi	28,681
9.	Jeypore	8	Koraput Nowrangpur Malkangiri	16,950
10.	Rayagada	5	Rayagada Boudh Kandhamal	12,910
	Total	**63**		**2,46,660**

Source: Compiled from the Records of the OSWC, Bhubaneswar.

The OSWC handles different commodities for storage as per the provision of the Warehousing Corporations Act, 1962. The main commodities received for storage in the warehouse are foodgrains and fertilizer. A small quantity of other commodities like cement, paper, oil, insecticides and other notified commodities are also received in some warehouses. Earlier, a major part of the capacity of warehouses was being utilized for storage of fertilizer. However, due to declining trend of fertilizer business, the foodgrain storage has increased considerably.

The OSWC has been rendering storage facility to as many as 38 depositors. However, the number of depositors utilizing the storage space varies from year to year depending upon the commodities accepted for storage in the warehouses. The important depositors are Food Corporation of India, State Civil Supplies Corporation, Agro-Industries Corporation, MARKFED, OPOLFED, OIL ORISSA, OFDC, Board of Secondary Education, TRIFED, NAFED, World-Food Programme Project, Seeds Corporation, State Trading Corporation, TDCC, Women and Child Development Department, CARE, Board of Revenue, NMEP, Text Book Press, District Medical Officers, District Social Welfare Officers, Fertilizer Companies like CF Ltd., FCI Ltd., IFFCO, IP Ltd., DMC Ltd., PP Ltd., PP and Ch Ltd., NFC Ltd., RCF Ltd., NF Ltd., Indo-Gulf Ltd., OSWAL, MMTC, Liberty Phosphates, G.S. Fertilizers, KRIBHCO Ltd., H.I. Ltd., R. P. Agro Chemicals, small and marginal farmers and traders etc.

Overall Performance of the OSWC during 1990's

The overall performance of the OSWC for a period of 10 years i.e. from 1990-91 to 1999-2000 is examined below. The performance evaluation of the OSWC is carried out in two aspects. They are: (i) physical performance and (ii) financial performance.

(i) Physical Performance

To analyse the physical performance of the Corporation the key physical parameters like capacity and utilization are taken into account. The percentage of utilization has been worked out and depicted in Table 3.2. It is observed from the table that during 1990-91, the average capacity of the OSWC was 1,88,699 metric tonnes of which 81.56 per cent was utilized. Thereafter, the capacity utilization showed a fluctuating trend ranging from 74.38 per cent in 1994-95 to 97.85 per cent in 1998-99. However, it is noticed from the table that the capacity utilization remained above 90 per cent during the year from 1996-97 to 1998-99. In other words, the capacity utilization of the OSWC was relatively better in the later years when compared to the early years of the study period. The year-wise capacity and utilization of warehouses of the OSWC is presented in Fig. 3.2.

TABLE 3.2

PHYSICAL PERFORMANCE OF THE OSWC

(in MT)

Year	*Average Capacity*	*Average Utilisation*	*Percentage of occupancy*
1990-91	1,88,699	1,53,908	81.56
1991-92	1,91,191	1,63,315	85.41
1992-93	1,95,665	1,58,857	81.18
1993-94	1,97,953	1,59,114	80.37
1994-95	1,92,002	1,42,814	74.38
1995-96	1,92,873	1,51,429	78.51
1996-97	2,23,113	2,15,018	96.37
1997-98	2,31,456	2,19,019	94.62
1998-99	2,38,258	2,33,136	97.85
1999-2000	2,40,126	2,09,870	87.39

Source: Compiled from the Annual Reports of the OSWC, Bhubaneswar.

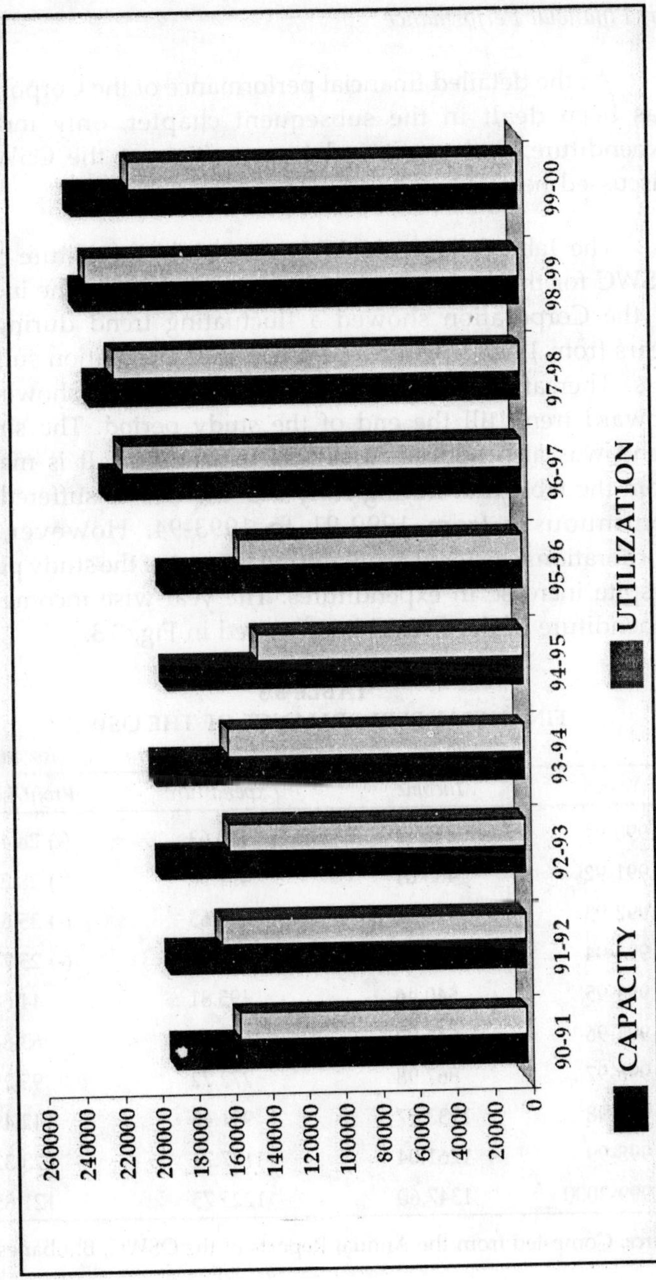
YEAR-WISE CAPACITY AND UTILIZATION OF GODOWNS OF THE OSWC
260000
240000
220000
200000
180000
160000
140000
120000
100000
80000
60000
40000
20000
0
90-91
91-92
92-93
93-94
94-95
95-96
96-97
97-98
98-99
99-00
CAPACITY
UTILIZATION

Fig: 3.2.

(ii) Financial Performance

As the detailed financial performance of the Corporation has been dealt in the subsequent chapter, only income, expenditure, and profit and loss position of the OSWC is discussed here.

The Table 3.3 reveals the income and expenditure of the OSWC for the period from 1990-91 to 1999-2000. The income of the Corporation showed a fluctuating trend during the years from 1990-91 to 1993-94 when the Corporation suffered loss. Thereafter, the income of the Corporation showed an upward trend till the end of the study period. The similar trend was also noticed in case of expenditure. It is marked from the table that during early 90s' the OSWC suffered loss continuously from 1990-91 to 1993-94. However, the Corporation registered profit during the rest of the study period despite increase in expenditures. The year-wise income and expenditure of the OSWC is presented in Fig. 3.3.

TABLE 3.3
FINANCIAL PERFORMANCE OF THE OSWC.

(Rs. in lakh)

Year	*Income*	*Expenditure*	*Profit/Loss*
1990-91	442.14	470.63	(-) 28.49
1991-92	423.01	451.30	(-) 28.28
1992-93	423.82	459.65	(-) 35.82
1993-94	420.01	445.79	(-) 25.77
1994-95	540.46	495.81	44.64
1995-96	645.92	582.08	63.84
1996-97	867.98	772.72	95.25
1997-98	1133.97	991.48	142.49
1998-99	1261.04	1137.71	123.32
1999-2000	1347.60	1225.75	121.85

Source: Compiled from the Annual Reports of the OSWC, Bhubaneswar.

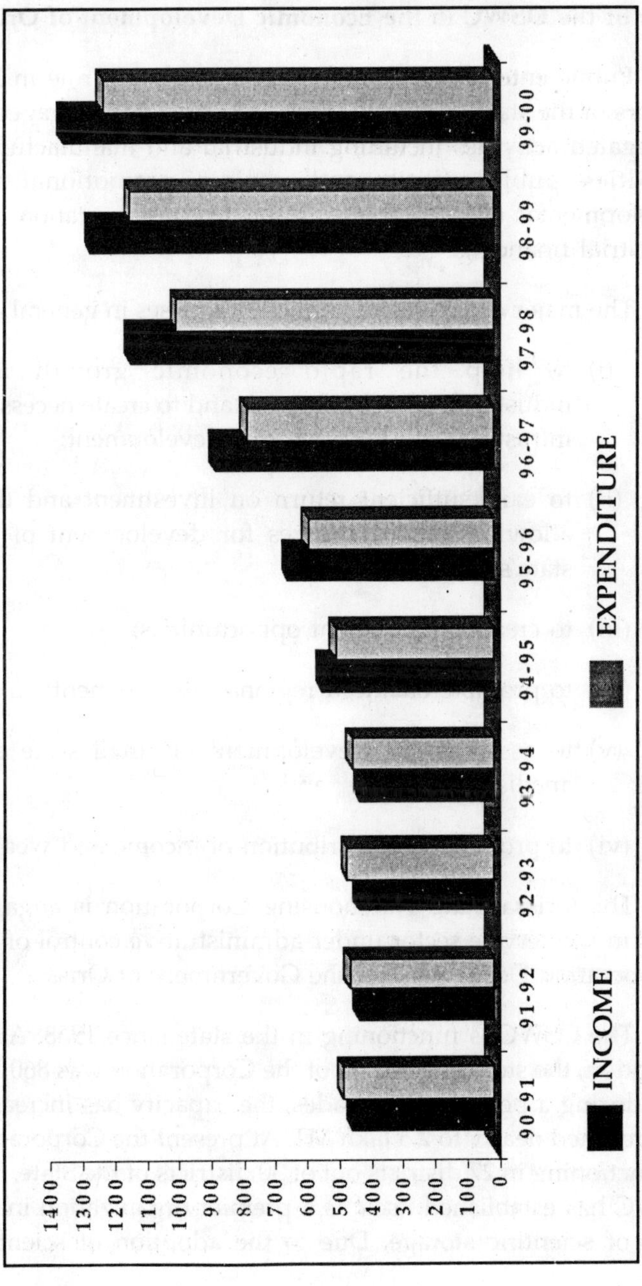
YEAR-WISE INCOME AND EXPENDITURE OF THE OSWC
1400
1300
1200
1100
1000
900
800
700
600
500
400
300
200
100
0
90-91
91-92
92-93
93-94
94-95
95-96
96-97
97-98
98-99
99-00
INCOME
EXPENDITURE

Fig: 3.3.

Role of the OSWC in the Economic Development of Orissa

Public enterprises are playing an important role in key sectors of the state economy. These enterprises are engaged in variegated activities including industrial and manufacturing activities, public utilities and services, promotional and developmental task, commercial and trading operation and industrial financing.

The major objectives of Public Enterprises in general are:

(i) to help the rapid economic growth and industrialization of the state and to create necessary infrastructures for economic development;

(ii) to earn sufficient return on investment and thus allowing extra resources for development of the state's economy;

(iii) to create employment opportunities;

(iv) to promote balanced regional development;

(v) to assist in the development of small scale and ancillary industries; and

(vi) to promote fair-distribution of income and wealth.

The Orissa State Warehousing Corporation is engaged itself in the service sector under administrative control of the Co-operation Department of the Government of Orissa.

The OSWC is functioning in the state since 1958. At its inception, the storage capacity of the Corporation was 860 MT and during a period of 4 decades, the capacity has increased and reached nearly to 2.5 lakh MT. At present the Corporation is functioning in 27 districts out of 30 districts of the State. The OSWC has established itself as a premier organization in the field of scientific storage. Due to the adoption of scientific storage and preservation techniques, storage loss of the stored commodities has been considerably reduced and thus it has minimized the colossal national loss.

The rural economy of the state is mainly dependent on the agriculture and allied activities. About 70 per cent of foodgrains remain with producers and others in villages for their use. The quantity that remains with the producers needs to be preserved well besides ensuring fair price for the same. On account of faulty methods of handling and storage of foodgrains about 10 per cent of the foodgrains are usually lost. The loss on account of defective storage alone has been estimated around 6.58 per cent[3]. It is observed that the storage loss at firm level, both qualitative and quantitative, are taking place during the post-harvest period. These losses are being minimized substantially by adopting scientific methods of storage at farm level and also by pursuing producers to store their produce in the OSWC godowns by paying nominal storage charges. In this way, the OSWC saves wealth of the nation and helps to add in the income of the producers.

Warehousing is intimately linked with credit and marketing. A licensed Warehouse In-charge can issue a warehouse receipt to the depositor. The banks accept the Warehouse Receipt as collateral security for grant of loans against goods stored in the warehouses. A warehouse receipt can be negotiable by endorsement and delivery. The producers are able to store their products in the Corporation's godowns during the harvest season and sell the produce at support price, thus avoiding distress sale. It is also helping them in securing commodity loans from the institutional sources at the prescribed rates of interest. Thus, the farmers are no longer remaining at the mercy of village money lenders. Their stocks are properly preserved and thus add value to their real income. Further the produce stored in the warehouses can be sold without much physical movement of stocks, and saves them from rough handling and also transport charges.

The banks are increasingly encourged in advancing commodity loans by accepting warehouse receipts as collateral security. This, in turn, helps the banking sector to do more business in rural areas. The consumers are getting foodstuffs at cheaper rates because of the elimination of loss in handling, transportation and storage. Apart from this, the traders are able to obtain loans from the banks and transact business through warehouse receipts on an increasing scale. The warehousing complexes are providing facilities for marketing of commodities within the framework of regulated markets, thus preventing undesirable and unscrupulous people from doing unfair practices to distort price. As a part of rural development and to transform the socio-economic conditions of the people in the rural areas, the Warehousing Corporation godowns are serving as centers for orderly distribution of essential commodities.

By associating the OSWC in public distribution system, it is ensuring distribution of qualitative foodstuffs to the public and also eliminating black marketers from public distribution system. The sufficient stocks in Corporation godowns has a psychological bearing on hoarding and other anti-social activities. Further, the Warehousing Corporation is of immense help to the Government of Orissa in times of emergencies like flood, cyclone, drought etc. to ensure timely availability of commodities for distribution and relief operations.

In areas like Sambalpur and Bargarh, which are considered as granaries of Orissa, the OSWC has constructed 28,200 MT capacity godowns and participated in the procurement process by assisting Government to avoid distress sale among the producers, more particularly the small and marginal farmers and millers. The OSWC is also planning to construct godowns having more capacities in the areas like Sambalpur, Bargarh, Bolangir, Kalahandi and Nuapara districts in the coming days.

In the remote areas of Kalahandi, Bolangir, Nuapada, Koraput, Rayagada, Nowrangpur, Malkangiri and Mayurbhanj districts, the OSWC has provided space to the depositors like

TRIFED, NAFED and Forest Department etc. for storage of forest products collected from the tribal people. As a result, the tribal communities are able to sell their products directly to the Government agencies by avoiding middlemen in the procurement process.

The Corporation has provided direct employment opportunities to 483 people, of which 468 are male and 15 are female employees. Out of the total staff, the strength of SC and ST are 51 and 24 respectively. That apart, about 2000 labourers have been engaged themselves directly or indirectly in the Corporation godowns spread over in 27 districts of the state. A large number of truck owners have also engaged their trucks for transportation of stocks from railhead to godowns point and also from godowns point to distance places, thus, helping in the easy availability of commodities in the remote corners of the state. As part of the diversification activities, the Corporation has engaged itself in clearing and forwarding works at Visakhapatanam and Paradeep Ports to generate more revenues for the developmental activities. The OSWC is contributing revenue regularly to the exchequer of the State Government and the Central Warehousing Corporation in shape of dividend barring a brief period.

From the above discussion it is very clear that the OSWC has directly or indirectly helped to enrich the economy of the state and in the coming years it is expected that the Corporation would significantly contribute to the economic development of the state.

SWOT Analysis of the OSWC

Strength, Weakness, Opportunities and Threats (SWOT) analysis is one of the primary steps in strategic management. Strategic management involves in the analysis of the organizational factors, i.e., the strength and weakness of the organization and the environmental factors i.e. the threats and opportunities in the business environment.

The strength and weakness of the Corporation has been examined by using the SWOT analysis taking into account the organisational and environmental factors. Further, necessary remedial measures have been suggested in the subsequent pages in order to strenghthen the warehousing system in the state. A brief note on the strength, weakness, opportunities and threats of the OSWC is presented below:

STRENGTH	WEAKNESS
❒ The OSWC was created by an Act of Parliament and has got the recognition of a Public Sector Corporation. ❒ Strong market presence in the sense that it is functioning from State Capital level to Panchyat level. ❒ Homogeneous storage practices. ❒ Established quality practices in identity-preserved storage. ❒ Can store a wide range of products in very large quantities ❒ Satisfactory record keeping and financial accounting ❒ Warehouse Receipts are accepted by almost all banks.	❒ Compared to production in the state, storage capacity is less, paving way to private warehousing. ❒ Utilisation of hired capacity to the tune of 1,02,409 metric tonnes resulting un-unscientific storage. ❒ High rate of handling and transport charges. ❒ Lack of communication facilities to the godowns located in the remote areas. ❒ Faulty recruitment policy. ❒ Redundant human resources. ❒ Excess manpower
OPPORTUNITIES	**THREATS**
❒ Large scale production and consumption of more chemical fertilizer in Agricultural sector ❒ New business aimed at shorter and cost-effective private supply chains. ❒ Partnerships and alliances with the private sectors. ❒ Alliances with banks and other lenders to channel credit to depositors. ❒ Increasing population ❒ Favourable change in depositors attitude.	❒ Large scale participation of private sectors in construction of storage facilities. ❒ Construction of godowns by public sectors like Food Corporation of India, Civil Supplies Corporation and MARKFED etc. ❒ Private warehousing. ❒ Uncertainties in climatic condition.

Prospects and Challenges

There is a notion that warehousing being a capital intensive industry, private capital is shy of investment in godown construction activity and hence the Warehousing Corporation has a monopoly in the field of warehousing. This does not hold good in the present context as Food Corporation of India is encouraging private parties to take up massive construction work in "Build Own and Operate" scheme. Likewise, public sector organizations like Food Corporation of India, Civil Supplies Corporation and Marketing Federation etc. are also constructing their own godowns for storage. As such, the Warehousing Corporation is going to face severe competition from other agencies (private and public sector) as well as private individuals. Now the industrialists are also thinking of entering into warehousing business as a part of their diversification programme. Therefore, the Warehousing Corporation will have to struggle hard for its existence. The future of the Warehousing Corporation may not be a bed of roses, unless diversification is attempted and enforced in a big way. An intensive drive and extensive spade of work is required so that in future Corporation's warehouses will provide a sort of regulated market inside the warehouse premises for both producers and consumers. The Warehousing Corporation in general and warehouses in particular should possess day to day market intelligence and keep a record of price trend so that the depositors can be kept informed of the trend and the OSWC can obtain their concurrence for the disposal of their goods. For this some sort of agency arrangement may be thought of and arranged with suitable and selected depositors in first instance. The samples of the customs available for such disposal can be exhibited in a prominent place in the warehouses for anybody to come and look at them.

In order to activate the warehousing business, an arrangement with fertilizer manufacturing companies can be made for distribution of fertilizer to the farmers directly from warehouses. Similarly distribution of cement, rice, edible oils and other essential commodities can also be taken up. The OSWC warehouses will have better opportunities since the warehouses are located throughout the state at various important trade centers even at block level.

From the foregoing discussion, it can be concluded that there are ample opportunities for expansion of warehousing business in the state. With the given know-how, expertise and experience, the Warehousing Corporation can march forward offering national service and social benefits to millions in the coming years.

References

1. S.C. Mohapatra, "Constitutional and Statutory Sketch of the Orissa State Warehousing Corporation", *Silver Jubilee Souvenir,* 1983, pp. 8-9.
2. Director of Census Operations, Orissa, *Census of India 2001, Series-22, Orissa, Paper 1 of 2001, Provisional Population Totals,* p. 1.
3. *Systems, Procedure and Practices of Scientific Warehousing,* Vol. I, Central Warehousing Corporation, New Delhi, 1982, p. 15.

Four

Analysis of Physical Performance of the OSWC

The Physical Performance of the Orissa State Warehousing Corporation from 1985-86 to 1999-2000 has been analyzed in the subsequent pages in order to know whether the Corporation was performing satisfactorily or not. Before analyzing the physical performance, an attempt has been made to examine different factors which have a direct bearing on it. The important factors, which are responsible for physical performance, are as follows :

(a) Location of godowns
(b) Capacity of godown
(c) Utilization of space
(d) Condition of godown
(e) Management of storage space
(f) Storage loss
(g) Quality of services
(h) Inspection and physical verification of warehouses, cleanlines, etc.

(a) Location of Godowns

The physical performance of the Corporation is directly dependent on the location of the godowns. The godowns situated near to market place or railway siding are the first choice of the users as they spend nominal amount towards transportation of their commodities. The Corporation is, therefore, giving much importance to establish its godowns in such locations for maximum utilization throughout the year.

(b) Capacity of Godown

Capacity of the warehouses is an important factor which indicates the volume of business transacted by the warehouses. The Orissa State Warehousing Corporation started its operation in the state by hiring two godowns having capacity of 860 MT in 1958. Since then, the capacity of the Corporation has increased over the years and the total capacity of the OSWC is 2,46,660 MT as on 31.03.2000. Out of this total capacity, the owned capacity is 1,64,350 MT and the hired capacity is 82,310 MT. The increase of capacity, both owned and hired, during last 15 years i.e. from 1985-96 to 1999-2000 made by the Corporation is highlighted below. Here, it is important to note that physical addition would reveal a positive sign on the overall performance of the Corporation.

(i) Owned Capacity

During the period from 1985-86 to 1999-2000, the Corporation has added modern scientific godowns of 1,09,600 MT in different parts of the state by spending an amount of Rs. 6.50 crore. The addition of warehouse capacity and the cost involved therein during last 15 years have been presented in the Table 4.1. From the table, it is noticed that the Corporation has added additional capacity throughout the study period except 1994-95. Further, it is noticed from the Table that the Corporation added more capacities during late Eighties. From the records, it is seen that these godowns were constructed mainly in procurement areas as well in the rural areas as a part of its developmental programme for the greater interest of the small and marginal farmers of the state.

TABLE 4.1
YEAR-WISE ADDITION OF NEW CAPACITY BY THE OSWC

Year	*Capacity (in MT)*	*Cost (Rs. in lakh)*
1985-86	13,500	63.89
1986-87	27,000	108.93
1987-88	14,000	65.75
1988-89	8,200	32.31
1989-90	9,800	42.84
1990-91	2,500	45.69
1991-92	9,100	62.50
1992-93	5,900	47.83
1993-94	2,600	15.24
1994-95	-	-
1995-96	5,000	32.25
1996-97	1,700	20.09
1997-98	800	9.46
1998-99	2,500	25.15
1999-2000	7,000	78.78
Grand Total	**1,09,600**	**650.71**

Source: Compiled from the Annual Reports of the OSWC, Bhubabeswar.

(ii) Hired Capacity

It can be said undoubtedly that the godowns available in Orissa is inadequate to store the foodgrains and other commodities. For instance, the procurement of rice in the state during 1999-2000 was about 9.00 lakh MT against which total godowns of the state was about 6 lakh MT only, thus showing a wide gap between production and storage. In order to bridge the gap the Corporation has been hiring the godowns from private parties. Another factor for hiring private godowns is that the construction of own godown is a time taking process and involves heavy outlay. However, soon after the liquidation of stock, the hired godowns are being de-hired on priority basis thus saving revenue for the Corporation. The Table 4.2 visualises the year-wise utilization of hired capacities by the OSWC during the study period. It is observed from the table that the Corporation has gradually reduced its dependence on hired godowns. This may be attributed to such reasons like the construction of owned godowns by the Corporation over the years on the one hand, and dehiring of unscientific hired godowns on the other hand.

TABLE 4.2
YEAR-WISE POSITION OF HIRED CAPACITIES OF THE OSWC

Year	*No. of warehouses*	*Hired capacity (in MT)*	*Variance*
1985-86	47	56,224	-
1986-87	50	69,012	(+) 12788
1987-88	56	89,358	(+) 20346
1988-89	58	72,884	(-) 16474
1989-90	67	64,133	(-) 8751
1990-91	67	59,366	(-) 4767
1991-92	71	58,805	(-) 561
1992-93	75	51,785	(-) 7020
1993-94	72	51,270	(-) 515
1994-95	72	44,302	(-) 6968
1995-96	72	44,756	(+) 454
1996-97	75	70,109	(+) 25353
1997-98	76	76,573	(+) 6464
1998-99	75	82,721	(-) 6148
1999-2000	67	81,001	(-) 1720

Source: Compiled from the Annual Reports of the OSWC, Bhubabeswar.

(c) Utilization of Space

The basic resource to be used in a warehouse is space. Therefore, proper utilization of space continues to be of utmost importance for the Corporation. The storage space is a cubic concept having length, breadth and height. Effective planning, thus, ensures full utilization of warehousing space.

Under one roof various commodities have to be stored and hence, it is required to follow different techniques with different codes of storage practices. The load bearing capacity of various goods accepted for storage are different and hence, very often stacking techniques as well as stack heights require changes. Therefore, proper management of storage space is vital not only to enhance the volume of stock but also to maximize the utilization of space.

(d) Condition of Godown

Basically an ideal godown is one which;

(a) protects the stock from ground moisture, rain, objectionable ordour, insects, rodent, birds and fire etc.

(b) provides necessary facilities for inspection, dis-infestation, loading, unloading, clearing and re-conditioning of agricultural commodities.

(c) is near to the grain market, railway siding, connected by good motorable road.

If these conditions are present then there is every possibility that the godowns are utilized fully and used throughout the year.

(e) Management of Storage Space

One of the main objectives of Warehousing Corporation is to decrease wastes and losses in storage by promoting and developing warehousing on scientific manner. In order to achieve this objective, the Corporation has taken a number of steps in this regard. The Corporation is providing scientific storage facilities to minimize losses during storage. The OSWC is the only organization in the state handling more than 200 agricultural and notified commodities. The commodities are preserved and protected from pest and vagaries of weather. The goods received at the warehouses are inspected, graded and weighed to determine the commercial quality and quantity. The Corporation undertakes the responsibility to return the same quantity of the goods to the depositors subject to normal shrinkage/dryness.

To achieve the main objectives of scientific storage the OSWC has laid down certain codes of storage practice as detailed below :—

(i) The stocks offered for storage are compulsorily analysed and graded as per the national grade.

(ii) For proper preservation of stock, orderly stacking has been introduced to facilitate inspection, physical verification, periodical disinfestation operations and proper aeration.

(iii) Fortnighly examination of stock is carried out to record the state of health and to undertake fumigation and other treatment, if necessary.

(iv) Prophylactic treatment is given to prevent cross infestation.

(v) Godown hygiene is maintained by regular cleaning and collection of spillages and other loose grains and segregating the damaged stocks from sound ones.

(vi) A small laboratory is provided in the warehouses with qualified and trained personnel to carry out these operations.

(vii) The stocks are stored by providing wooden crate/ polythene sheets/bamboo mats as dunnage to prevent seepage of floor water during storage.

The above measures are adopted with a view to provide scientific storage, maintain the marketable and nutritive value of the goods to fetch premium price in the market even after storing for a considerable period. Thus, a sense of interest is created among the depositors to store their products in the godowns of the Corporation with a view to get higher premium for their produce.

(f) Storage Loss

As discussed earlier, one of the main objectives of the Warehousing Corporation is to decrease wastages and losses during storage. Keeping this objective in mind, the OSWC is working hard to minimize the losses during storage by adopting scientific storage practices in the warehouses.

In the post-harvest stages, it has been estimated that due to faulty methods of handling, storage and movement of goods, 9.33 per cent of the production is lost. The loss during storage alone is 6.58 per cent. Due to the adoption of scientific storage and preservation practices, storage losses, particularly while storing grain commodities, have been reduced substantially. The storage losses as revealed from the records of the OSWC show that as against normal loss of 6.58 per cent, the loss during storage of foodgrains in the godowns of the OSWC is minimal, i.e., less than 1 per cent. Thus, the OSWC has contributed in a big way in preventing the post-harvest losses.

(g) Quality of Services

The Corporation has been giving top most priority to customer's service. The slogan of the OSWC is "a customer is the most important visitor on the OSWC premises. He is not dependent on him rather the OSWC is dependent on him". With this concept, the OSWC has inculcated a sense of belongingness among its employees who are working for the organization relentlessly from the morning to the late evening hours. That apart, the OSWC is giving utmost priorities in scientific maintenance of the stock accepted for storage to minimize loss during storage. Customer relationship and industrial relation is maintained for smooth operation in the warehouses of the OSWC.

(h) Regular Inspection and Physical Verification of Stock

In order to have an effective control over the warehousing administration and for the satisfaction of the customers, periodical inspections and physical verifications including surprised visits by the senior officers are being conducted. Inspection and physical verification means checking of godown hygiene, physical verification of stock and cash account of a warehouse. Regular inspection keeps the warehouse incharge and his staff always alert. Because of the correct maintenance of stock accounts the depositors are expressing their confidence on the OSWC.

From the foregoing discussion, it can be concluded that the performance of the warehouses in general and the OSWC in particular chiefly depends upon a number of factors. If these factors are taken care of, it is needless to say that the well-being of the Corporation is ensured and it will revolutionize the warehousing business in the state.

Evaluation of Key Physical Parameters

In order to evaluate the physical performance of the OSWC, the key physical parameters, namely, number of warehouses, capacity– hired and constructed, utilization of warehouses by different depositors and commodity-wise utilizaton of warehouses, etc. are taken into account. The rational idea behind the evaluation is to assess whether the OSWC is performing well or otherwise. A detailed analysis on various parameters are outlined below.

Storage Capacity and Utilization

The storage capacity of the OSWC and their utilization for a period of 15 years are presented in Table 4.3. It is observed from the table that during 1985-86, the Corporation had only 47 warehouses having a total capacity of 1,25,924 MT, of which 69,700 MT was the owned capacity and 56,224 MT was the hired capacity. The share of owned and hired capacity were 55.35 per cent and 44.65 per cent respectively. However, the number of warehouses had gone up in the subsequent years. The number of warehouses were 76 during 1997-98 having a total capacity of 2,31,456 MT. However, the number of warehouses was reduced to 67 during 1999-2000, but the capacity of the warehouses increased to 2,40,126 MT. This is mainly due to expansion of existing warehouses. The capacity of owned godowns and hired godowns increased to 1,59,125 MT and 81,001 MT respectively by the end of March, 2000. In other words, the owned and hired capacity of the Corporation increased by 2.28 and 1.44 times respectively during a period of 15 years.

TABLE 4.3
STORAGE CAPACITY UTILIZATION OF THE OSWC

(in MT)

Year	No. of warehouses	Capacity			Capacity utilization	% utilization
		Own	Hired	Total		
1985-86	47	69700	56224	125924	139805	111.02
1986-87	50	82542	69012	151554	158672	104.69
1987-88	56	104767	89358	194125	202792	104.46
1988-89	58	113072	72884	185956	164992	88.72
1989-90	67	123940	64133	188073	163286	86.82
1990-91	67	129333	59366	188699	153908	81.56
1991-92	71	132306	58805	191191	163315	85.41
1992-93	75	143880	51785	195665	158857	81.18
1993-94	72	146683	51270	197953	159114	80.37
1994-95	72	147700	44302	192002	142814	74.38
1995-96	72	148117	44756	192873	151429	78.51
1996-97	75	153004	70109	223113	215018	96.37
1997-98	76	154883	76573	231456	219019	94.62
1998-99	75	155533	82721	238258	233136	97.85
1999-2000	67	159125	81001	240126	209870	87.39
CAGR		6.08%	2.71%	4.78%	3.02%	

Source: Compiled from the Annual Reports of the OSWC, Bhubaneswar.

The total capacity utilization of the warehouses reveals a fluctuating trend during the study period. It is also noticed that though the number of warehouses and capacity have increased over the years yet the year to year comparison of capacity and utilization reveals a low rate of growth in capacity utilization. It is evident from the compounded average growth rate (CAGR) figures that the CAGR for capacity utilization is 3.02 per cent, where as the CAGR for capacity is 4.78 per cent druing the study period. The reason behind this under utilization of capacity is due to the opening of a very small capacity godowns like 50 MT to 200 MT in remote villages as a part of the OSWC's service oriented obligation to the rural masses in the orderly distribution of commodities under Public Distribution System (PDS) as per the directions of the State Government from time to time. It is pertinent to note here that even though small godowns have been taken for PDS, the same could not be utilized fully. Apart from that, the normal godowns have also not been utilized fully due to non-availability of custom and business patronage which caused lower percentage of occupancy. The year-wise position on own capacity and hired capacity utilization have been depicted in Fig. 4.1 for the period of our study.

Month-wise Utilisation of Storage Space

To get an idea on the working of the Corporation in utilization of the space, a detailed analysis with month-wise occupation from 1995-96 to 1999-2000 has been worked out and depicted in Table 4.4.

In analyzing the month-wise figures, it is noticed that there is no clear-cut trend in the utilization of space. In order to get an idea with regard to month-wise performance, the entire period i.e. one year has been divided into 3 sub-periods namely :—

(i) Occupancy from April to September;

(ii) Occupancy from October to December; and

(iii) Occupancy from January to March.

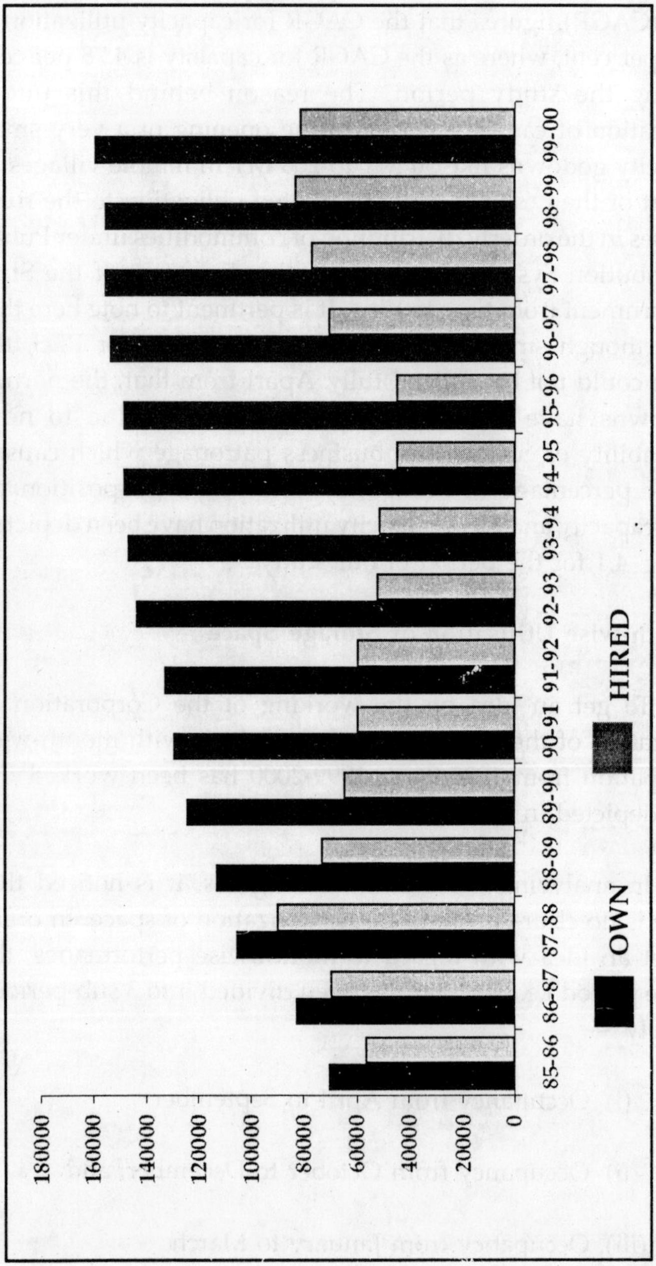
YEAR-WISE POSITION ON OWN AND HIRED CAPACITY OF THE OSWC
180000
160000
140000
120000
100000
80000
60000
40000
20000
0
85-86
86-87
87-88
88-89
89-90
90-91
91-92
92-93
93-94
94-95
95-96
96-97
97-98
98-99
99-00
OWN
HIRED

Fig: 4.1.

TABLE 4.4
MONTH-WISE UTILIZATION OF STORAGE CAPACITY OF THE OSWC

(in lakh MT)

Month	*1995-96*			*1996-97*			*1997-98*			*1998-99*			*1999-2000*		
	Capa-city	*Utili-zation*	*%*	*Capa-city*	*Utili-zation*	*%*	*Capa-city*	*Utili-zation*	*%*	*Capa-city*	*Utili-zation*	*%*	*Capa-city*	*Utili-zation*	*%*
April	1.87	1.44	77	2.20	2.35	107	2.31	2.22	96	2.31	2.38	103	2.36	2.24	95
May	1.90	1.56	82	2.28	2.64	116	2.39	2.37	99	2.38	2.76	116	2.36	2.24	95
June	1.93	1.60	83	2.32	2.67	115	2.40	2.55	106	2.43	2.92	120	2.42	2.24	93
July	1.92	1.49	78	2.31	2.50	108	2.40	2.50	104	2.47	2.82	114	2.41	2.25	93
August	1.89	1.38	73	2.25	2.21	98	2.38	2.36	99	2.48	2.57	104	2.40	2.20	92
September	1.88	1.37	73	2.22	2.00	90	2.32	2.11	91	2.43	2.38	98	2.39	2.11	88
October	1.89	1.24	66	2.16	1.80	83	2.26	1.86	82	2.36	2.07	88	2.36	1.75	74
November	1.89	1.27	67	2.13	1.57	74	2.27	1.81	80	2.35	1.92	82	2.35	1.76	75
December	1.90	1.38	73	2.14	1.71	80	2.25	2.00	89	2.31	1.84	80	2.40	1.83	76
January	1.92	1.59	83	2.19	2.00	91	2.25	2.09	93	2.75	2.04	87	2.46	2.12	86
February	2.00	1.82	91	2.25	2.12	94	2.25	2.16	96	2.36	2.14	91	2.44	2.12	92
March	2.13	2.00	94	2.31	2.22	96	2.27	2.24	99	2.35	2.11	90	2.47	2.20	89
Average	**1.92**	**1.51**	**79**	**2.23**	**2.15**	**96**	**2.31**	**2.19**	**95**	**2.38**	**2.33**	**98**	**2.40**	**2.09**	**87**

Source: Compiled from the Annual Reports of the OSWC, Bhubaneswar.

The table shows that the occupancy position during April to September was ranging from 73 per cent to 120 per cent and likewise, the occupancy position during October to December was ranging from 66 per cent to 98 per cent. The range of occupancy position during January to March was in between 83 per cent and 99 per cent.

While interacting with the management personnel at the field level, it is ascertained that during April to September the fertilizer stocks are received for storage in the godowns for utilization by the farmers for khariff crops. However, after the delivery of the same, and due to non receipt of further fertilizer stocks during October to December, the occupancy position usually remains at the lower side. Similarly, during the procurement season i.e. from January to March again the occupancy increases considerably.

From the above analysis, it is clear that the utilization of godown space largely depends on deposits of fertilizer stocks as well as procurement of foodgrains in the state. Moreover, utilization of godown space is purely seasonal. The peak period of utilization of warehouse godowns is normally during January to March. It is followed by a period of moderate utilization i.e. from April to September. The lean period remains during October to December, when the godown space remain un-utilized due to non-deposit of stock by various users.

Zone-wise Distribution of Capacity and Occupancy

The zone-wise analysis has been made to know how efficiently the warehouses in different zones were utilised during the study period. In order to understand this the zone-wise capacity and occupancy has been worked out from 1995-96 to 1999-2000 and depicted in Table 4.5. The table reveals that during 1995-96 only seven zones, namely Jagatpur, Cuttack, Berhampur, Sambalpur, Titilagarh, Jeypore and Kayagada, were functioning. Out of seven zones, the Titilagarh

TABLE 4.5
ZONE-WISE DISTRIBUTION OF CAPACITY AND OCCUPANCY OF WAREHOUSES OF THE OSWC

(in thousand MT)

Name of the Zones	1995-96 Capacity in MT			1995-96		1996-97 Capacity in MT			1996-97		1997-98 Capacity in MT			1997-98		1998-99 Capacity in MT			1998-99		1999-2000 Capacity in MT			1999-2000	
	Own	Hired	Total	Avg. occu-pancy	% of occu pancy	Own	Hired	Total	Avg. occu-pancy	% of occu pancy	Own	Hired	Total	Avg. occu-pancy	% of occu pancy	Own	Hired	Total	Avg. occu-pancy	% of occu pancy	Own	Hired	Total	Avg. occu-pancy	% of occu pancy
Jagatpur	29.50	-	29.50	29.37	99.55	29.50	-	29.50	32.91	111.55	29.50	-	29.50	33.72	114.30	29.50	-	29.50	32.46	110.03	29.50	-	29.50	33.20	112.54
Cuttack	24.10	6.59	30.69	32.03	104.36	24.10	10.67	34.77	33.56	96.51	6.50	7.50	14.00	11.11	79.35	6.50	7.51	14.01	9.95	71.02	10.20	6.42	16.62	9.22	55.47
Berhampur	19.50	14.98	34.48	29.73	86.22	20.00	21.92	41.92	40.94	97.66	20.00	19.89	39.89	40.27	100.95	20.00	26.61	46.61	45.35	97.29	7.00	12.93	19.93	13.03	65.37
Sambalpur	31.90	10.10	42.00	38.73	92.21	33.60	6.85	40.45	35.56	87.91	34.40	4.05	38.45	26.25	68.27	34.44	3.94	38.34	20.88	54.46	32.20	2.89	35.09	30.10	85.77
Titilagarh	25.00	20.49	45.48	43.30	95.20	25.75	22.09	47.84	45.88	95.90	25.75	24.67	50.44	55.30	109.63	25.75	26.79	52.54	52.80	100.49	22.25	13.34	35.59	36.87	103.59
Jeypore	14.20	1.93	16.13	12.42	76.99	14.20	6.28	20.48	18.43	89.99	14.20	4.61	18.81	16.20	86.12	14.20	3.94	18.14	15.67	86.38	14.20	2.75	16.95	11.06	65.25
Rayagada	8.50	7.11	15.61	14.49	92.82	7.00	9.17	16.17	17.96	111.06	7.00	6.29	13.29	14.80	111.36	9.50	4.99	14.49	11.71	80.81	10.00	2.91	12.91	10.07	78.00
Balasore	-	-	-	-	-	-	-	-	-	-	17.60	5.62	23.22	26.57	114.42	17.60	4.19	21.79	21.78	99.95	18.60	4.28	22.88	22.52	98.42
Bhubaneswar	-	-	-	-	-	-	-	-	-	-	-	-	-	-	-	-	-	-	-	-	14.40	14.09	28.49	24.86	87.25
Bhawani-patna	-	-	-	-	-	-	-	-	-	-	-	-	-	-	-	-	-	-	-	-	6.00	22.68	28.68	29.52	102.92
Average	152.7	61.2	213.89	200.07	93.53	154.15	76.98	231.13	225.24	97.45	154.95	72.63	227.6	224.22	98.51	157.49	77.97	235.42	210.6	89.45	164.35	82.29	246.64	220.45	89.38

Source: Compiled from the Annual Reports of the OSWC, Bhubaneswar.

zone had the highest capacity of 45.48 thousand MT. Balasore zone was created during 1997-98 and, similarly another two new zones, namely Bhubaneswar and Bhawanipatna, were formed in 1999-2000. Thus, the total number of zones were ten as on March, 2000 while it was seven during 1995-96. The three additional zones were created by bifurcating the warehouses which previously remained under Cuttack, Berhampur, Titilagarh and Sambalpur zones.

While interacting with the management personnel, it is inferred that the new zones were created from the point of view of administrative conveniences and commercial benefits. It is also marked that even after the creation of three new zones, the Titilagarh zone continued to be the highest provider of warehousing facilities. Further, it is marked from the table that the Corporation has added more capacity in Sambalpur zone followed by Jagatpur zone. Similiarly, the Corporation had utilized more hired godowns in the Titilagarh zone till 1998-99 and, thereafter, Bhawanipatna zone took the lead in utilizing the hired godowns to the extent of 22.86 thousand MT.

With regard to percentage of occupancy in different zones, it is seen that Jagatpur zone handled more stock and maintained more than 100 per cent occupancy during 1995-96 to 1999-2000. Similarly, Titilagarh zone also maintained about 100 per cent occupancy on an average during the study period. Though, Cuttack zone utilized fully its storage capacity during 1995-96 to 1996-97, later the occupancy percentage showed a sharp decline. The percentage of utilization of space in Berhampur, Sambalpur, Jeypore and Rayagada zones marked a fluctuating trend throughout the study period. Another interesting feature known from the table is that after the creation of new zones, the Bhawanipatna zone achieved more than 100 per cent occupancy. The Balasore and Bhubaneswar zones, however, maintained 98.42 per cent and 87.25 per cent occupancy respectively as on 31.3.2000.

With regard to percentage of occupancy in different zones, it is seen that Jagatpur, Titilagarh, Balasore and Bhawanipatna zones utilized the space more efficiently than the other zones. Poor utilization of stock/space has been marked in Cuttack, Jeypore and Berhampur zones. The reason for such low occupancy was due to non-receipt of fertilizer stocks from fertilizer companies and foodgrains from Food Corporation of India.

District-wise Distribution of Capacity and Occupancy

In order to know the occupancy position of each district, the capacity and utilization of each district has been estimated. The Table 4.6 shows the district-wise break-up of capacity, average occupancy and percentage of occupancy of State Warehouses as on 31st March, 2000. From the table, it is noticed that Cuttack district has the highest warehousing capacity of 35,870 MT followed by Kalahandi district with 28,681 MT. The average occupancy position shows that Cuttack had handled stock of 37,427 MT followed by Kalahandi with 29,526 MT. However, so far as the percentage of occupancy position is concerned, Kendrapara district utilized warehousing facilities to the extent of 151.27 per cent followed by Malkanagiri with 135.29 per cent. It is also observed from the table, that Jagatsinghpur, Boudh and Khandhamal districts had the distinction of providing the least storage facility to the extent of nil, 8.40 per cent and 9.42 per cent respectively. On the whole, Cuttack, Balasore, Bhadrak, Kendrapara, Gajapati, Sambalpur, Bolangir, Kalahandi and Malkangiri districts handled more stock as compared to the facilities available in the warehouses.

It is further observed that during 1985-86, the Corporation was functioning in all the 13 districts. However, after creation of new districts, the number of districts in the State of Orissa increased to 30. At present the Corporation is functioning in 27 districts. The districts which are not yet covered by the OSWC are Deogarh, Dhenkanal and Sonepur. However, attempts are being made by the Corporation to open warehouses in these districts either by hiring or constructing godowns of its own.

TABLE 4.6
DISTRICT-WISE BREAK-UP OF CAPACITY AND OCCUPANCY OF WAREHOUSES OF THE OSWC

(As on 31st March, 2000)

Name of the District	*Capacity in MT*			*Average occupancy in MT*	*% of Occu-pancy*
	Own	*Hired*	*Total*		
Cuttack	30,500	5,370	35,870	37,427	104.34
Jagatsinghpur	1,000	-	-	-	-
Jajpur	3,500	500	4,000	2,132	53.30
Keonjhar	1,000	-	1,000	180	18.00
Kendrapara	-	550	550	832	151.27
Angul	3,700	-	3,700	1,858	50.21
Balasore	7,100	1,742	8,842	11,459	129.59
Bhadrak	6,500	2,543	9,043	9,287	102.69
Mayurbhanja	5,000	-	5,000	1,779	35.58
Puri	1,500	1,575	3,075	1,957	63.64
Khurda	12,900	13,197	26,097	23,329	89.39
Ganjam	5,000	11,142	16,142	9,578	59.33
Nayagarh	1,000	-	1,000	488	48.80
Gajapati	1,000	1,111	2,111	2,539	120.27
Sambalpur	8,500	200	8,700	9,328	107.21
Bargarh	19,700	1,290	20,990	18,262	87.00
Sundargarh	500	1,400	1,900	655	34.47
Jharsuguda	3,500	-	3,500	1,861	53.17
Bolangir	18,250	6,660	24,910	26,371	105.86
Nuapara	4,000	6,689	10,689	10,500	98.23
Kalahandi	6,000	22,681	28,681	29,526	102.94
Koraput	4,000	1,000	5,000	1,960	39.20
Nowranghpur	8,700	400	9,100	5,244	57.62
Malkangiri	1,500	1,350	2,850	3,856	135.29
Rayagada	8,500	2,710	11,210	9,923	88.51
Boudh	1,000	-	1,000	84	8.40
Phulbani	500	200	700	66	9.42

Source: Compiled from the Annual Reports of the OSWC, Bhubaneswar.

Category-wise Warehouses and Utilization

The godowns of the OSWC are categorized under four heads namely, 'A', 'B', 'C' and 'D' on the basis of the capacity of the godowns. The 'A' category warehouse has the capacity of 10,000 MT and above. The capacity of the 'B', 'C' and 'D' categories of warehouses are in the range of 5000 MT to 9999 MT, 1000 MT to 4999 MT and below 1000 MT respectively.

From the records of the OSWC, it is found that there are 6 numbers of 'A' category warehouses in the state. The total capacity of these warehouses are 90,489 MT, which constitutes 36.68 per cent of the total capacity as on 31.03.2000. Similarly, there are 14 warehouses under 'B' category having a total capacity of 94,171 MT, which constitutes 38.18 per cent of the total capacity. Likewise, 23 warehouses under 'C' category are available with a total capacity of 52,431 MT which represent 21.86 per cent of the total capacity. The 'D' category godowns numbering 20 have a total capacity of 9,569 MT which constitutes only 3.88 per cent of total capacity.

From the Table 4.7 it is revealed that out of 6 'A' category warehouses, Nagenpali warehouse has utilized the maximum capacity i.e. 118.68 per cent as on 31st March, 2000. Whereas the Berhampur warehouse utilized only 65.32 per cent of the capacity as on the same date.

With regard to 'B' category warehouses the Table 4.8 shows that the maximum utilization of warehouse was Balasore with 135.55 per cent and the minimum utilization of warehouse was Jagannathpur with 49.31 per cent of the total available capacity as on 31st March, 2000. In case of 'C' category warehouses, the Table 4.9 furnishes information that, except few warehouses, the percentage of utilization was very poor in most other warehouses. However, in case of 'D' category warehouses as shown in Table 4.10 it is marked that except few warehouses the percentage of utilization in most of the other warehouses was moderate.

TABLE 4.7
'A' CATEGORY WAREHOUSES - CAPACITY AND OCCUPANCY
as on 31st March, 2000.

Name of the warehouses	*Capacity in MT*	*Average occupancy in MT*	*% of Occupancy*
Jagatpur	29,500	33,201	112.54
Jatni	10,009	9,563	95.54
Berhampur	10,695	6,986	65.32
Nagenpali	11,000	13,055	118.68
Khariar Road	10,689	10,500	98.23
Kesinga	18,596	19,161	103.03
Total	**90,489**	**92,466**	**102.18**

Source: Compiled from the Annual Reports of the OSWC, Bhubaneswar.

TABLE 4.8
'B' CATEGORY WAREHOUSES - CAPACITY AND OCCUPANCY
as on 31st March, 2000

Name of the warehouses	*Capacity in MT*	*Average occupancy in MT*	*% of Occupancy*
Cuttack	5,370	4,141	77.11
Balasore	8,060	10,926	135.55
Bhadrak	8,543	9,194	107.62
Bhubaneswar	7,400	6,158	83.21
Khurda	8,011	7,183	89.66
Jagannathpur	5,037	2,484	49.31
Durgapali	8,700	9,328	107.21
Attabira	7,290	4,451	61.05
Bolangir	9,050	10,513	116.16
Kantabanji	5,600	5,870	104.82
Malmunda	5,000	5,270	105.40
Junagarh	5,400	6,775	125.46
Gunupur	5,500	7,195	130.81
Rayagada	5,210	2,728	52.36
Total	**94,171**	**92,216**	**97.92**

Source: Compiled from the Annual Reports of the OSWC, Bhubaneswar.

TABLE - 4.9
'C' CATEGORY WAREHOUSES - CAPACITY AND OCCUPANCY

as on 31st March, 2000

Name of the warehouses	*Capacity in MT*	*Average occupancy in MT*	*% of Occupancy*
Banki	1,000	85	8.50
Jagatsinghpur	1,000	-	-
Dhanmandal	3,500	1,630	46.57
Keonjhar	1,000	180	18.00
Angul	3,200	1,858	58.06
Baripada	2,500	907	36.28
Rairangpur	1,500	286	19.06
Nimapara	1,575	1,363	86.53
Sakhigopal	1,500	594	39.60
Paralakhemundi	2,111	2,539	120.27
Barpali	2,700	756	28.00
Rourkela	1,400	495	35.35
Nayagarh	1,000	488	48.80
Jharsuguda	3,500	1,861	53.17
Titilagarh	4,260	4,618	108.40
Bhawanipatna	2,735	2,890	105.66
Narla Road	1,250	-	-
Jeypore	4,500	1,445	32.11
Kotpad	1,000	470	47.00
Umerkote	3,100	2,057	66.35
Nowrangpur	4,500	2,717	60.37
Malkangiri	2,600	3,582	137.76
Boudh	1,000	84	8.40
Total	**52,431**	**30,905**	**58.94**

Source: Compiled from the Annual Reports of the OSWC, Bhubaneswar.

TABLE 4.10
'D' CATEGORY WAREHOUSES - CAPACITY AND OCCUPANCY

as on 31st March, 2000

Name of the warehouses	*Capacity in MT*	*Average occupancy in MT*	*% of Occupancy*
J. K. Road	500	502	100.40
Kendrapara	550	832	151.27
Talcher	500	-	-
Nilagiri	500	336	67.20
Haldipada	282	197	69.85
Chandbali	500	93	18.60
Karanjia	500	86	17.20
Udala	500	500	100.00
Balugaon	677	425	62.77
Aska	410	108	26.34
Sundargarh	500	160	32.00
Mahadevpali	500	-	-
S. Rampur	500	100	20.00
Charbahal	300	300	100.00
Jaipatna	400	400	100.00
Borigumma	500	515	103.00
Raighar	500	-	-
Mathili	250	274	109.60
Jemedipeta	500	-	-
Phulbani	700	66	9.42
Total	**9,569**	**4,894**	**51.14**

Source: Compiled from the Annual Reports of the OSWC, Bhubaneswar.

From the above analysis, it is observed that 'A' and 'B' category warehouses constitute the major portion of the total storage capacity. These two categories of godowns jointly shared 76.91 per cent of the total capacity. As regards to occupancy, these category of godowns on an average utilized the capacity fully as on 31.3.2000. The 'C' category godowns, having capacity of 52,431 MT have only utilized up to 30,905 MT. In other words, the 'C' category godowns utilized only 58.94 per cent of the total capacity. Similarly 'D' category godowns having capacity of 9,569 MT utilized only 4,894 MT which was only 51.14 per cent of the total capacity.

Depositor-wise Utilization of Warehousing Facilities

The warehousing facilities are generally used by the State Government Departments/Organizations, Food Corporation of India, Fertilizer Companies, Co-operative Institutions/Organizations, farmers and traders. The depositor-wise occupancy of the Corporation's warehouses for a period of 15 years i.e. from 1985-86 to 1999-2000 is presented in Table 4.11.

It is seen from the table that the Food Corporation of India and the Fertilizer Companies are the major utilizers of the warehouses of the Corporation. A close look into the table reveals that the Fertilizer Companies occupied first place in utilizing the warehouses of the Corporation during the years from 1985-86 to 1990-91. However, since 1991-92 the trend reversed and the Food Corporation of India took the first place in utilizing the warehousing facilities. On an average, the Food Corporation and the Fertilizer Companies shared 41.05 per cent and 34.64 per cent respectively of the total utilized capacity during the study period. The depositor-wise utilization of warehousing facilities is shown in Fig. 4.2.

TABLE 4.11
DEPOSITOR-WISE OCCUPANCY OF WAREHOUSES OF THE OSWC

(in MT)

Year	State Govt. Deptt./ Organisation	Percentage	Food corpn. of India	Percentage	Fertiliser companies	Percentage	Co-operatives	Percentage	Farmers	Percentage	Traders & others	Percentage	Total	Percentage
1985-86	21796	15.59	54328	38.86	48554	34.73	4096	2.93	1580	1.13	9451	6.76	139805	100
1986-87	23595	14.87	36272	22.86	86889	54.76	5522	3.48	5918	3.73	476	0.30	158672	100
1987-88	41775	20.60	62054	30.60	92068	45.40	2636	1.30	2028	1.0	2231	1.10	202792	100
1988-89	39070	23.68	45191	27.39	77134	46.75	66	0.04	1980	1.20	1551	0.94	164992	100
1989-90	22860	14.00	39189	24.00	93073	57.00	6531	4.00	1306	0.8	327	0.20	163286	100
1990-91	26164	17.00	56946	37.00	62333	40.50	5387	3.50	2309	1.5	769	0.50	153908	100
1991-92	34296	21.00	68593	42.00	37562	23.00	16332	10.00	1633	1.0	4899	3.00	163315	100
1992-93	38968	24.53	68340	43.02	32296	20.33	16314	10.27	1430	0.90	1509	0.95	158857	100
1993-94	31266	19.65	78618	49.41	31902	20.05	13843	8.70	923	0.58	2562	1.61	159114	100
1994-95	23280	16.30	74412	52.10	26565	18.60	15711	11.00	714	0.5	2142	1.50	142824	100
1995-96	28772	19.00	70868	46.80	34829	23.00	14855	9.81	560	0.37	1545	1.02	151429	100
1996-97	35263	16.40	106004	49.30	66656	31.00	2580	1.20	1720	0.8	2795	1.30	215018	100
1997-98	50988	23.28	86119	39.32	74292	33.92	4183	1.91	569	0.26	2869	1.31	219020	100
1998-99	33595	14.41	114283	49.02	80246	34.42	863	0.37	606	0.26	3543	1.52	233136	100
1999-2000	12382	5.90	121725	58.00	68627	32.70	1050	0.50	1679	0.8	4407	2.10	209870	100
Average	30938	17.60	72196	41.05	60869	34.64	7331	4.17	1664	0.95	2738	1.56	1,75,736	100
CAGR	-ve		5.94%		2.56%		-ve		-ve		-ve		3.02%	

Source: Compiled from the Annual Reports of the OSWC, Bhubaneswar.

Depositor-wise Occupancy of Warehouses of the OSWC

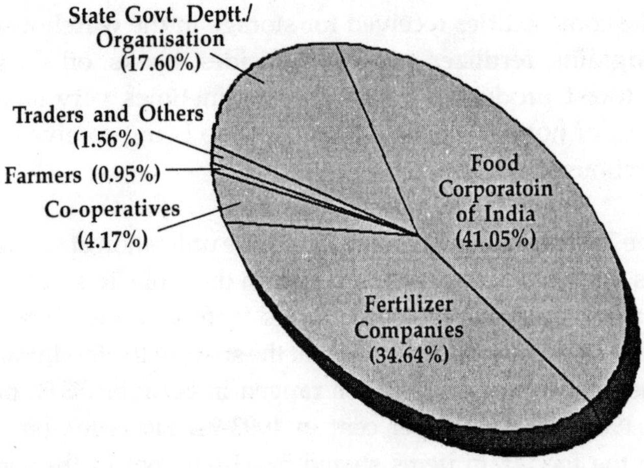

Fig. 4.2.

It is noteworthy to mention here that, one of the functions of the Corporation is to stabilize the agricultural prices and to expand institutional agricultural credit through the Warehouse Receipts. But the occupancy position of the farmers shows a discouraging note, i.e., the farmers have utilized the warehousing facilities less than 1 per cent on an average during the study period. As a result, the very purpose of the Warehouse Receipt mostly remained unfulfilled. Similarly, the space utilization made by the traders shows a dismal note during the study period. The traders and others utilized on an average 1.56 per cent of the total utilized capacity during the study period. An analysis of the compounded average growth rate reveals that the depositors like Food Corporation of India and Fertilizer Companies registered positive growth rate of 5.94 per cent and 2.56 per cent respectively during the study period. While the rest depositors recorded negative growth (CAGR). From the above analysis, it can be inferred that the government agencies and the big business houses are the major users of the warehousing facilities.

Commodity-wise Utilization of Warehousing Facilities

The commodities received for storage in the warehouses are foodgrains, fertilizer, papers, pesticides, books, oil seeds, pulses, forest products etc. However, sometimes very small quantities of notified commodities are also being received in the warehouses.

The Table 4.12 shows commodity-wise utilization of storage facilities from 1985-86 to 1999-2000. From the table, it is noticed that maximum capacity has been utilized for foodgrains followed by fertilizer. Further, it is observed that the share of the foodgrains from the total capacity utilization ranged in between 38.80 per cent in 1989-90 to 69.64 per cent in 1993-94. However, on an average the foodgrain items shared 59.63 per cent of the total utilized capacity during the study period.

The occupancy position of fertilizer item has remained next to foodgrains. During 1989-90, while a maximum of 57% of the total capacity was occupied by fertilizer the minimum of 18.60% was noticed of it during 1994-95. The average percentage of utilization of space by fertilizer item during the study period is 34.64 per cent. The foodgrains and fertilizer combinedly utilized on an average 94.27 per cent of the available space during the study period. The balance 5.73% of space was utilized by other products. This is evident from the growth rate (CAGR) made by the foodgrains and the fertilizer during the study period which were 4.07 per cent and 2.56 per cent respectively. The commodity-wise average utilization of storage facilities during the study period has been presented through Pie-chart (Fig. 4.3).

From the foregoing analysis, it can be stated that the total capacity of the warehouses of the Coporation has not been fully utilized during most of the years of the study period.

TABLE 4.12
COMMODITY-WISE UTILIZATION OF THE WAREHOUSES OF THE OSWC

Year	*Foodgrains*	*Percentage*	*Fertilizer*	*Percentage*	*Others*	*Percentage*	*Total*	*Percentage*
1985-86	77704	55.58	48554	34.73	13547	9.69	139805	100
1986-87	65785	41.46	86889	54.76	5998	3.78	158672	100
1987-88	105857	52.20	92068	45.40	4867	2.40	202672	100
1988-89	86241	52.27	77134	46.75	1617	0.98	164992	100
1989-90	63355	38.80	93073	57.00	6858	4.20	163286	100
1990-91	85419	55.50	62333	40.50	6156	4.00	153908	100
1991-92	104522	64.00	37562	23.00	21231	13.00	163315	100
1992-93	108738	68.45	32296	20.33	17823	11.22	158857	100
1993-94	110807	69.64	31902	20.05	16405	1031	159114	100
1994-95	98406	68.90	25565	18.60	17853	12.50	142824	100
1995-96	100200	66.17	34829	23.00	16400	10.83	151429	100
1996-97	142987	66.50	66656	31.00	5375	2.50	215018	100
1997-98	137676	62.86	74292	33.92	7052	3.22	219020	100
1998-99	148484	63.69	80246	34.42	4406	1.89	233130	100
1999-2000	135786	64.70	68627	32.70	5457	2.60	209870	100
Average	104798	59.63	60868	34.64	10070	5.73	175736	100
CAGR	4.07%		2.56%		-ve		3.02%	

Source: Compiled from the Annual Reports of the OSWC, Bhubaneswar.

Commodity-wise Utilization of the Warehouses of the OSWC

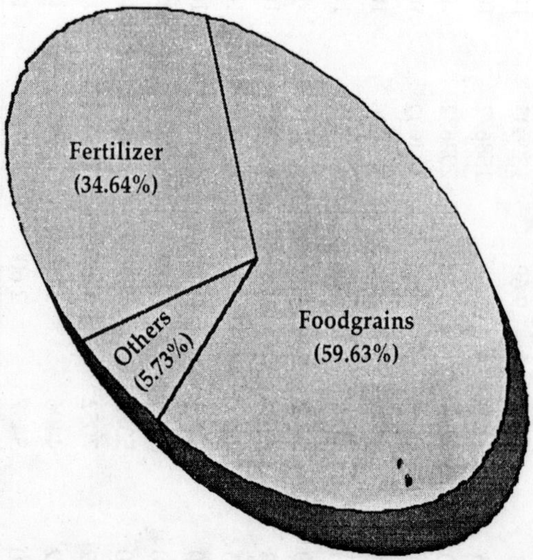

Fig. 4.3.

Further, the season-wise occupation reveals that during April to September, the occupancy position of warehouses is relatively better than the the remaining months. The occupancy position in different zones depicts that Balasore, Kalahandi, Titilagarh, Jagatpur, Khurda, Gajapati, Nuapara and Malkangiri have handled more stocks in their warehouses. The warehousing facilities are largely utilized by Food Corporation of India and Fertilizer Companies. Both the organizations jointly account for 73.59 per cent of the total available storage capacity. The cooperatives, farmers and traders utilized the remaining 26.41 per cent storage facilities. Similarly, the commodity-wise occupancy position reveals that foodgrains and fertilizer jointly utilized 94.27 per cent of the warehouse space.

Five

Analysis of Financial Performance of the OSWC

Accounting figures are dumb. However, if analyzed, they may tell a vivid story of the financial adventures of an enterprise. Financial analysis is a scientific evaluation of the profitability and financial strength of any business concern. Financial statement analysis attempts to unveil the meaning and significance of the items composed in profit and loss account and balance sheet so as to assist the management in the formulation of sound operating financial policies. A great deal of knowledge can be had about business performance and financial position through an appraisal of financial statements. Financial analysis is the process of making an analytical study of the financial and operational data contained in the profit and loss account and the balance sheet of a given concern and thereby satisfying the information needs of the internal and external users of such data. An analysis of both these statements gives a comprehensive understanding of business operations and their impact on the financial health.[1] The appraisal or analysis of financial statements spotlights the significant facts and relationship concerning managerial performance, corporate efficiency, financial strength and weakness and credit worthiness that would have otherwise been buried in a maze of detail.[2] Thus, the financial analysis is a preliminary step towards the financial evaluation of the results drawn by the analysts. The analysis of such results is made by the management for decision making process. Keeping this in view, the present chapter examines the operational efficiency, profitability, solvency both short term and long term etc. of the Orissa State Warehousing Corporation.

Financial analysis is the end of a continuous flow of accounting cycle which starts from classification, recording, summarizing, presentation and analysis of data and ends with the interpretation of the results obtained from such an analysis. Thus, the analysis and interpretation of financial statements are an attempt to determine the meaning and significance of the financial statement data so that a forecast may be made of the prospects for future earnings, ability to pay interest and debt maturities (both current and long term) and profitability of a sound dividend policy.[3] These statements are valuable in the sense that they depict how the financial data of the related enterprise fit into the fabric for its accounting system. It aids in decision making to various users interested in the financial status and operating results of the business. According to Moore, "financial analysis is a process synthesis and summarization of financial and operative data embodied in the financial statements with a view to get an insight into the operative activities of a business enterprise".[4] It is a technique of X-raying the financial position as well as the progress of the company.[5]

As noted above, the major and most significant financial statements of a business concern are the profit and loss account and the balance sheet. A careful examination of profit and loss account throws ample light on the operating efficiency, inventory management, control over indirect overheads and dividend policies perused by the concern. Moreover, a study of the major individual items of a statement in relation to some other items of other statement will measure the activity and the profitability of the enterprise. As both of the major financial statements are interrelated, the analysis of only either of them is devoid of the purpose.

Meaning of Financial Statements

Although any formal statement expressed in money values might be thought of as financial statements, the term has come to be limited by most accounting and business writers to mean the 'balance sheet' and the 'profit and loss statement'.[6] The principal financial statements include the balance sheet, the income statement and the statement of retained earnings of a business enterprise. The balance sheet is also known as the statement of assets and liabilities. The balance sheet may be defined as a statement prepared with a view for measuring the financial position of a business enterprise at a given date. From the analyst's point of view a balance sheet is a written representation of the resources and liabilities of an individual, a partnership, an association or a corporation.[7] In fact, the balance sheet reflects the financial position of a concern only at a particular point of time i.e. the last day of the accounting year.

The profit and loss account also known as income statement is the schedule that shows the incomes and expenses of a business over a period of time and gives a final figure representing the amount of profit or loss for the accounting period.[8] The period of time may be one year but it is a period of time rather than a moment of time as in the case of the balance sheet.

From the above, it can be said that balance sheet reflects the financial position of a concern only at a particular point of time, i.e. the last day of the accounting year. In this sense, the balance sheet may be regarded as a photo camera of the financial position of a concern. On the other hand, the profit and loss account is an abstract portrayal of the dynamic life of the business presenting a longitudinal picture of the gains and losses of the business, its fortunes and misfortunes.[9]

Objectives of Financial Statement Analysis

The financial statements are intended to give an accurate picture of a concern's financial condition and operating results in a condensed form. The overall objective of a business is to earn a satisfactory return on the funds invested in it, consistent with maintaining a sound financial position.[10] The objective of financial analysis is a detailed cause and effect study of the profitability and financial position.[11] The success of an investment depends ultimately upon future developments and the future may never be analyzed with accuracy. But if you have precise information as to a company's present financial position and its past earnings record, you are better equipped to gauge its future possibilities.[12] The available information can be crystallized in such a way that its implications are classified and attention can be concentrated upon facts which are in the usual balance sheet and profit and loss account, completely hidden behind a mass of figures.[13] However, the analysis of financial statements cannot give an absolute answer to every question of doubt it may bring to light but it can and will point to the direction in which further enquiries should be made.

The objectives of financial statement analysis are different for different users of information viz., management, investors, creditors, labour, government and others. They are as follows.

(i) Management

Analysis of financial statements helps the management to study the relative efficiency of different departments. They are able to spot weaknesses in the company's operations and can take corrective action. It tends to restrain management, as they are under pressure to maintain a favourable financial position.

(ii) Investors

The investors are primarily interested with the safety of their investment and the ability of the company to generate profit. By analysing financial statements, the prospective investors can take investment decision.

(iii) Creditors

The creditors are primarily concerned with the solveny and credit worthiness of the concern. Analysis of financial statements help them in knowing whether the company is in a position to honour obligations (payment of interest and repayment of principal) as and when they mature.

(iv) Government

Government regulates economic activities in various spheres and for this purpose analysis of financial statements of companies in one industry or of all companies is very helpful. Earning ratios and turnover ratios are used as barometer to indicate the health of an industry as a whole.

(v) Employees

Employees have an interest in the operating results and the financial strength of a company. The remuneration of the employees must be generated from the company revenues. Thus, the employees' wages, to a great extent, depends upon the success of the firm. Employees' demand for more wages and salaries, thus, depend on the financial position of the concerned unit which can be known from the financial statements. Hence, the ability of the company to meet the higher wages and salaries of employees can be studied from the information provided in the financial statements.

Apart form the above stated groups, the trade association, labour bureaus, research institutions, stock exchanges etc. are also keenly interested in the results arrived at by analysis of financial statements to know the progress being made and the present position of an industry.

Process of Analysis of Financial Statements

The process of analysis of financial statements involves the compilation, comparison and study of financial data and the preparation, study and interpretation of measuring devices such as ratios, trends and percentages.[14] The first step in this direction is the reorganization and rearrangement of the entire financial data as embodied in the financial statements. By such reclassification, the profit and loss account and the balance sheet are completely recast and presented in a condensed form which become entirely different from their original shape. A large amount of financial data is thus reduced to a simple, analytical and standard form. The second step is the establishment of significant relationships between the individual components of profit and loss account and the balance sheet through the application of tools of financial analysis. In the third step, the significance of comparative data obtained by applying tools of financial analysis is evaluated. Finally, the comparative data so arrived in the previous step is compared with the standard in order to know the performance of the concerned unit. Here the standards so fixed enable the analyst in understanding the sound as well as unsound relationship as reflected by the comparative data. In other words, the relative magnitude is judged in the light of these standards. Then the information is interpreted in simple and understandable way along with its significance so as to help in decision making. Specific conclusions arrived at as a result of financial analysis are presented in the form of a report which highlight the financial position of the concern. However, the precision in the result of financial analysis depends upon the skill, judgment and experience of the analyst.

Techniques of Financial Statement Analysis

In order to analyze the financial statements a number of tools and techniques are available with the analyst. The important techniques namely ratio analysis, common-size statement analysis, comparative statement analysis, trend analysis, funds flow analysis, etc., are used to analyse the financial statements to know the operational and financial performance of the organization. Besides, the statistical techniques like standard deviation, coefficient of variation, correlation, regression, analysis of time series, index number etc. are also used along with financial techniques to provide more scientific analysis. As stated above, there are various financial tools and techniques to analyse the financial statements. However, in the present study only the ratio analysis technique is used to analyse the financial statements of the OSWC in order to know its operational and financial performance. Before utilizing the ratio analysis as a tool of financial statement analysis, it is felt essential to discuss its meaning, objective and significance.

Ratio Analysis

Ratios are among the best known and most widely used tools of financial analysis. It is the principal technique used in judging the condition portrayed by the financial statements. An analyst can judge by its use the financial growth, development and the present position of a business enterprise. A ratio is simply one number expressed in terms of another. It is found by dividing one number, the base into the other. Ratios are simply a means of highlighting in arithmetical terms the relationship between figures drawn from financial statements.[15] Ratios may be expressed in either of the three forms : (i) a pure ratio, e.g., 2:1, (ii) as a rate, i.e., in times and (iii) as percentage.

The term 'accounting ratios' is used to describe significant relationship which exists between figures shown in a balance sheet, in a profit and loss account, in a budgetary control system or in any other part of the accounting organization.[16] When the relationship between two figures of the balance sheet is established the ratio thus calculated is called 'balance sheet ratio'. Similarly, when the relationship between the figures of profit and loss account is established, the result so found is regarded as 'income statement ratio'. It is not merely limited to establish the relationship or calculation of ratios but the ratio analysis is the process of determining and interpreting numerical relationship based in financial statements. The analyst with the help of the ratio analysis technique can diagnose the financial condition of the concern. If the condition is found adverse, suitable timely measures can be taken up to overcome it. The ratio analysis provides guides and clues especially in spoting trends towards better or poor performance and in finding out significant deviation from any average or relatively applicable standard.[17]

Generally, financial ratios are analyzed in two ways : (i) time series analysis, and (ii) cross-section analysis. Time series analysis indicates the behaviour and movement of a given ratio overtime. In cross-section analysis, the investigated ratio is evaluated in relation to a representative ratio of the industry for the same period.[18] Thus, the basic objective of time series analysis is to evaluate the trend of a ratio(s), while the cross-section analysis points out any deviation in the representative ratio value by comparing it with the standard. In both types of analysis, it can take one of the following forms: static determination and analysis and/or dynamic adjustment and its analysis.[19] The static determination of financial ratios involves the calculation and analysis of ratios over a number of periods for one company or the analysis of differences in ratios among the individual firms in one industry. In dynamic analysis, regression of current ratios against past ratios is made to analyse the dynamic nature and the adjustment process of a firm's ratio. This is helpful to compare companies with one another and find out the strength and weakness of performance of a concerned unit. In dynamic analysis the adjustment process can be made either through single equation dynamic adjustment method or simultaneous determination method. The latter method assumes greater importance as it embodies a combination of financial circumstances.[20]

Classification of Ratios

Ratios are classified in different ways. One way of classifying the ratios is the source from which it is drawn such as balance sheet ratio, profit and loss account ratio and combined ratio. The other way of classifying the ratio is on the basis of what they indicate, the symptoms or characteristics namely, liquidity, profitability, financial stability and turnover relationship etc.[21] However, the latter classification assumes greater significance because it speaks distinctly the different aspects of business performance and helps the various users of financial statements to take guard of their interest. For instance, short term creditors are interested to evaluate the liquidity position by analyzing the liquidity ratios while the long term creditors and investors are interested in the solvency and profitability position of the organization and as such they study the solvency and profitability ratios. The different categories of ratios along with their significance are discussed in the following section.

As already observed that ratio analysis is by far the most widely used method of financial statement analysis. It carries a number of advantages. They are :

(i) It simplifies the comprehension of financial statements. Ratios tell the whole story of changes in the financial condition of the business;

(ii) It provides inter-firm comparison to measure efficiency and helps the management to take corrective action;

(iii) A ratio trend helps in planning and forecasting; and

(iv) It helps in the investment decision to make profitable investment.

Thus, ratio can assist management in its basic functions of forecasting, planning, coordination, controlling and communicating.[22]

Despite the utility of ratio analysis, it may not be a precise technique for ascertaining liquidity, solvency and profitability position of a firm. It is because of the dissimilarities of firms in an industry with regard to business policy, accounting procedures, management policy and knowledge of the persons preparing such statements. Hence, it is difficult to establish a standard ratio of the industry for comparison. Thus, any comparison of actual ratio with the standard ratio may give misleading information. Another limitation of ratio analysis is that it cannot take into the uncertainities of future and other economic changes while making a projection of ratio trend. Inspite of the above limitations, the ratio analysis is considered as a potential technique for evaluating the financial performance of an undertaking.

A detailed analysis of financial performance of the OSWC with regard to its liquidity, profitability, solvency etc. is carried out in the following paragraphs.

Liquidity Ratios

Liquidity refers to the ability of a firm to meet its obligations in the short run, usually one year. Liquidity ratios measure the ability of the firm to meet its current obligation.[23] A firm should ensure that it does not suffer from lack of liquidity and also that it does not have excess liquidity. The failure of a firm to meet its obligations due to lack of sufficient liquidity will result in a poor credit worthiness, loss of creditor's confidence, or even in legal tangles resulting in the closure of the firm. A very high degree of liquidity is also bad because idle assets earn nothing. The firm's funds will be unnecessarily tied-up in current assets. Therefore, it is necessary to strike a proper balance between high liquidity and lack of liquidity.

The most common ratios which indicate the extent of liquidity or lack of it are- (i) current ratio, and (ii) quick ratio. The liquidity position of the OSWC is examined through current ratio and quick ratio in the following paragraphs.

(i) Current Ratio

The current ratio is calculated by dividing current assets by current liabilities. The formula for computation of current ratio is given below.

$$\text{Current ratio} = \frac{\text{Current assets}}{\text{Current liabilities}}$$

Current assets include cash, and those assets which can be converted into cash within a year, and also include cash and bank balances, marketable securities, inventory, debtors net of provision for bad and doubtful debts, bills receivables and prepaid expenses. The current liabilities are those liabilities which are short-term maturing obligations, as originally contemplated within a year. This consists of trade creditors, bills payables, bank credit, provision for taxation, dividends payable and outstanding expenses.

The current ratio of a firm measures its short-term solvency, i.e., its ability to meet short-term obligations. As a measure of short-term solvency, it indicates the rupees of current assets available for each rupee of current liability.

Apparently, the higher the current ratio, the greater the short term solvency and vice-versa. Conventionally, a current ratio of 2:1 (current assets twice of current liabilities) is satisfactory. The logic underlying the conventional rule is that even with a drop-out of 50 per cent (half) in the value of the current assets, a firm can still meet its obligations, i.e., a 100 per cent margin of safety is assumed to be sufficient to ward off the worst situations.

The rule of thumb (a current ratio of 2:1) cannot, however, be applied mechanically. The satisfactory current ratio will differ depending on the development of the capital market and availability of long term funds to finance current assets. Another factor which has a bearing on the current ratio is the nature of business. For instance, public utility firms generally have a very low current ratio. Normally such firms have very little need for current assets.

Thus, the standard norm of current ratio (2:1) may vary from firm to firm. However, a ratio of less than 1:1 would certainly be undesirable in any unit because at least some safety margin is required to protect the interest of the creditors and to provide cushion to the firm in adverse circumstances.

The current ratio for a period of 15 years of the Orissa State Warehousing Corporation is presented in Table 5.1. The current ratio of the OSWC was 1.7:1 in 1985-86 which declined to 0.9:1 in 1993-94. Thereafter, it marginally increased and remained above 1:1 in the rest of the study period. A close look into the table reveals that the current ratio was higher in the early part of the study period as compared to the rest of the study period. The fall in the current ratio in the later years was due to more increase in current liabilities than the current assets. However, the Corporation maintained an average current ratio of 1.08:1 during the study period. The coefficient of variation of the two series i.e. curent assets and current liabilities are 48.49 and 50.53 respectively and they have positive correlation of high degree (r = 0.98). The variation in current liabilities is slightly higher than the current assets. The high degree of positive correlation shows that the Corporation has followed a uniform policy to finance current assets and current liabilities.

TABLE 5.1
CURRENT RATIO OF THE OSWC

(Rs. in lakh)

Year	*Current assets*	*Current liabilities*	*Current ratio*
1985-86	369.47	219.45	1.7:1
1986-87	395.68	264.27	1.5:1
1987-88	491.20	349.38	1.4:1
1988-89	566.97	474.26	1.1:1
1989-90	679.93	599.28	1.1:1
1990-91	881.77	863.31	1.02:1
1991-92	834.07	860.64	0.9:1
1992-93	859.67	928.39	0.9:1
1993-94	975.05	1042.98	0.9:1
1994-95	1008.42	1005.38	1:1
1995-96	1052.98	1035.94	1.01:1
1996-97	1224.99	1186.83	1.03.1
1997-98	1602.04	1422.49	1.12:1
1998-99	1615.97	1420.61	1.13:1
1999-2000	1965.45	1764.29	1.11:1
Average	968.24	895.83	1.08:1
S. D.	469.48	452.68	—
C.V.	48.49	50.53	—
r	—	—	0.98

Source: Compiled from the Annual Reports of the OSWC, Bhubaneswar.

It can be noted here that the short term solvency position of the Corporation was favourable during the early part of the study period than the later part where it became relatively unfavourable.

(ii) Acid-test/Quick Ratio

From the above discussion, it appears that all types of current assets have equal value so far as liquidity is concerned. For instance, a rupee of cash is considered equivalent to rupee of inventory or receivable. But it is not so. A rupee of cash is more liquid to meet current obligations than a rupee of, say, inventory. Hence, it weakens the usefulness of the current ratio.

The acid test ratio is a measure of absolute liquidity which is designed to overcome the defect of current ratio. Acid test ratio is also known as quick ratio, because it converts such current assets quickly into cash to meet the current liabilities.

The acid test ratio is the ratio between quick current assets and current liabilities and is calculated by dividing the quick assets by the current liabilities.

$$\text{Acid test ratio} = \frac{\text{Quick assets}}{\text{Current liabilities}}$$

An asset is said to be quick / liquid if it can be converted into cash within a short period without loss of value. In that sense, cash in hand and cash at bank are the most liquid assets. The other assets which are included in the liquid category are bills receivables, sundry debtors, marketable securities and short term or temporary investments. Inventories cannot be converted into cash immediately without a sufficient loss of value. In the same manner, pre paid expenses are also excluded from the list of quick assets because they are not expected to be converted into cash quickly.

The acid test ratio of the OSWC has been worked out and depicted in Table 5.2. The quick ratio of the Corporation was 1.7:1 in 1985-86. Thereafter, the quick ratio values declined and remained at 0.9:1 in 1993-94. However, a marginal increase was noticed during the rest of the study period. Like current ratio, the quick ratio was more favourable during the early part of the study period as compared to the rest of the study period. A close look into the figures of the quick ratio of the entire study period shows that the Corporation was comfortably placed as its quick ratio was remained more or less at 1:1. In other words, the absolute liquidity position of the Corporation was satisfactory during the study period.

TABLE 5.2
ACID TEST RATIO OF THE OSWC

(Rs. in lakh)

Year	*Quick assets*	*Current liabilities*	*Quick ratio*
1985-86	368.85	219.45	1.7:1
1986-87	395.17	264.27	1.5:1
1987-88	490.69	349.38	1.4:1
1988-89	566.47	474.26	1.1:1
1989-90	679.43	599.28	1.1:1
1990-91	881.27	863.31	1:1
1991-92	833.56	860.64	0.9:1
1992-93	859.16	928.39	0.9:1
1993-94	974.54	1042.98	0.9:1
1994-95	1007.91	1005.38	1:1
1995-96	1052.47	1035.94	1:1
1996-97	1224.48	1186.83	1.1:1
1997-98	1601.53	1422.49	1.1:1
1998-99	1615.47	1420.61	1.1:1
1999-2000	1964.95	1764.29	1.1:1
Average	967.73	895.83	1.08:1
S.D.	469.49	452.68	—
C.V.	48.51	50.53	—
r	—	—	0.98

Source: Compiled from the Annual Reports of the OSWC, Bhubaneswar.

The above analysis on the liquidity position of the Corporation clearly states that the short term solvency was satisfactory during the study period except three years, i.e. from 1991-92 to 1993-94. Further, there was no much difference between current ratio and quick ratio values because the share of inventory in the total current assets of the Corporation was very less. Again it can be noted that the coefficient of variation and coefficient of correlation figures of current ratio and quick ratio are more or less same.

Solvency/Leverage Ratios

Financial leverage refers to the use of debt finance. While debt capital is a cheaper source of finance, it is also riskier source of finance.[24] Leverage ratios help in assessing the risk arising from the use of debt capital. Two types of ratios are commonly used to analyse financial leverage: Structural ratios and Coverage ratios. Structural ratios are based on the proportions of debt and equity in the financial structure of the firm. Coverage ratios show the relationship between debt servicing commitment and the sources of meeting these burdens. Leverage ratios are used to judge the long-term financial position of the firm. In other words, it is a measure to determine the financial risk and the firm's ability of using debt for the benefit of owners.

Leverage ratio is calculated from the balance sheet items to determine the proportion of debt in total financing. Many variations of these ratios exist. The leverage ratio indicates the extent to which the firm has relied on debt in financing its assets. To study the long term solvency position of the OSWC, the important ratios namely debt equity ratio, total debt ratio and interest coverage ratio are analysed in the following pages.

(i) Debt-Equity Ratio

Debt-equity ratio is calculated to measure the relative claims of outsiders and shareholders against the firm's assets. The relationship between borrowed funds and owner's capital is a popular measure of the long-term financial solvency of a firm. This ratio indicates the relative proportions of debt and equity in financing the assets of a firm. The relationship between outsider's claim and owner's capital are shown in different ways and accordingly, there are many variants of debt-equity ratio.

One approach is to express the debt-equity ratio in terms of the relative proportion of long-term debt and shareholders equity. The formula used to calculate the debt-equity ratio is as follows.

$$\text{Debt-Equity (D/E) ratio} = \frac{\text{Long-term debt}}{\text{Shareholder's equity}}$$

The debt-equity ratio is the ratio of total outside liabilities to owners' total funds. In other words, it is the ratio of the amount invested by the outsiders and the owners of business. The debt-equity ratio is an important tool of financial analysis to appraise the financial structure of a firm. A high ratio of debt-equity means a large share of finance provided by the creditors to the firm and like-wise a low ratio implies a small quantum of fund given by creditors. The debt-equity ratio indicates the margin of safety available to the creditors. If debt-equity ratio is 1:2, it implies that for every rupee of outside liability, the firm has two rupees of owner's capital or the stake of the creditors in the business is half of the owner's. Conversely, if the debt-equity ratio is 2:1, it implies more stake but low safety margin for the creditors.

The purpose of debt-equity ratio is to get an idea of the cushion available to outsiders in the event of liquidation of the firm. As a general rule, there should be an appropriate mix of owner's fund and outsider's fund in financing the firm's assets. The interpretation of debt-equity ratio depends primarily upon the financial policy of a firm and firm's nature of business.

A ratio of 1:1 usually considered to be a satisfactory ratio although there is no 'rule of thumb' or standard norm for all types of business. In some business, a high ratio of 2:1 or even more is considered satisfactory. Generally, a low ratio (debt being low in comparison to shareholder's funds) is considered as favourable to long-term creditors because it provides a high margin of safety to them. A high debt-equity ratio on the other hand gives a lesser margin of safety to them.

The debt-equity ratio of the OSWC is computed and shown in Table 5.3. In analyzing the debt-equity ratio of the Orissa State Warehousing Corporation it is seen that the debt-equity ratio depicted a downward movement during the study period. The debt-equity ratio of the Corporation was 1.36:1 during 1985-86. Thereafter, it reduced consistently and remained at 0.10:1 during 1998-99. The Corporation maintained a debt-equity ratio of 0.70 :1 on an average during the study period. The coefficient of correlation of debt-equity being highly negative (-0.79) indicates that the Corporation could not maintain a uniform policy to finance the debt and equity capital. On the other hand, with decline in the induction of borrowed capital, the Corporation has been deprived of taking the advantage of leverage especially during the later part of the study period.

(ii) Total Debt Ratio

The total debt ratio is a variant of debt-equity ratio used to analyse the long-term solvency of a firm. Some times, the firm is interested to know the proportion of the interest bearing debt in its capital structure. The debt ratio can be computed by dividing total debt by capital employed. Total debt includes short and long term borrowings, deferred payment arrangements for purchasing capital equipments, public deposits and any other interest bearing loan. Capital employed includes total debt and net-worth.

$$\text{Total debt ratio} = \frac{\text{Total debt}}{\text{Total debt + Net worth}}$$

TABLE 5.3
DEBT-EQUITY RATIO OF THE OSWC

(Rs. in lakh)

Year	*Long-term debt*	*Shareholders equity*	*Debt-equity ratio*
1985-86	217.63	158.96	1.36:1
1986-87	217.04	176.96	1.22:1
1987-88	233.99	191.96	1.21:1
1988-89	216.27	205.96	1.05:1
1989-90	209.31	210.96	0.99:1
1990-91	197.82	232.96	0.84:1
1991-92	187.07	242.96	0.76:1
1992-93	198.87	251.48	0.79:1
1993-94	205.10	260.00	0.78:1
1994-95	175.66	300.00	0.58:1
1995-96	159.22	300.00	0.53:1
1996-97	129.86	300.00	0.43:1
1997-98	88.21	300.00	0.29:1
1998-99	33.51	320.00	0.10:1
1999-2000	-	320.00	—
Average	176.39	251.48	0.70:1
S. D.	56.77	52.35	—
C. V.	32.18	21.23	—
r	—	—	-0.79

Source: Compiled from the Annual Reports of the OSWC, Bhubaneswar.

The total debt ratio of the Orissa State Warehousing Corporation has been depicted in Table 5.4. It is seen from the table that there had been continuous rise in the quantum of debt proportion from 0.48:1 in 1985-86 to 0.70:1 in 1993-94. However, thereafter a slow or marginal decline in debt amount was marked till the end of the study period. The average debt ratio of the Corporation was calculated at 0.65:1 during the study period.

TABLE 5.4
TOTAL DEBT RATIO OF THE OSWC

(Rs. in lakh)

Year	*Total debt*	*Total debt+Net worth*	*Total debt ratio*
1985-86	219.45	456.82	0.48:1
1986-87	264.27	555.95	0.47:1
1987-88	349.39	709.81	0.49:1
1988-89	474.26	864.19	0.55:1
1989-90	599.28	993.70	0.60:1
1990-91	863.31	1273.17	0.68:1
1991-92	860.65	1280.51	0.67:1
1992-93	928.40	1356.78	0.68:1
1993-94	1042.98	1479.88	0.70:1
1994-95	1005.39	1482.29	0.68:1
1995-96	1035.95	1512.85	0.68:1
1996-97	1186.83	1743.73	0.68:1
1997-98	1422.49	2132.89	0.67:1
1998-99	1420.61	2244.01	0.63:1
1999-2000	1764.30	2684.70	0.66:1
Average	895.83	1384.75	0.65:1
S.D.	452.68	632.64	-
C.V.	50.53	45.69	-
r	-	-	0.99

Source: Compiled from the Annual Reports of the OSWC, Bhubaneswar.

In other words, the lenders have financed on an average 0.65:1 of the Corporaiton's net assets. It is observed from the table that the Corporation used more debt finance in the latter part of the study period. A close look into the table further reveals that both the debt as well as net worth of the Corporation were in the rising order. However, the rise in debt was relatively more than the rise in net worth of the Corporation during the study period.

It is evident from the coefficient of variation and the coefficient of correlation figures that the total debt and the capital employed of the Corporation moved in the same direction. However, the rise in total debt can be attributed to more induction of short-term borrowings. The foregoing analysis states that the Corporation used only limited amount of fixed interest bearing securities and did not take advantage of leverage.

Interest Coverage Ratio

The second category of leverage ratio is the coverage ratio. The leverage ratios discussed above are static in nature and fail to indicate the Corporation's ability to meet interest obligations. The interest coverage ratio is one of the most conventional coverage ratios used to test the firm's debt-servicing capacity. The interest coverage ratio shows the number of times the interest charges are covered from the earnings that are available with the firm. Since, taxes are computed after payment of interest, interest coverage is calculated in relation to before tax earnings. The interest coverage ratio is computed by dividing Earning Before Interest and Taxes (EBIT) by interest charges.

$$\text{Interest coverage ratio} = \frac{\text{EBIT}}{\text{Interest}}$$

Interest coverage ratio indicates the number of times interest is covered by the earnings available to pay the interest charges. It also indicates the extent to which the earnings may fall without causing any embarrassment to the firm regarding payment of interest charges. A higher ratio is desirable; but too high a ratio indicates that the firm is conservative in using debt and that it is not using credit to the best advantage of shareholders. A low ratio indicates excessive use of debt or inefficient operation. Therefore, the firm should make efforts to improve the operating efficiency or to retire debt to have a comfortable coverage ratio.

The interest coverage ratio of the Orissa State Warehousing Corporation is calculated and depicted in Table 5.5. In analyzing the interest coverage ratio of the Orissa State Warehousing Corporation, it is seen that the coverage ratio during 1985-86 to 1989-90 were in between 1.98 times and 3.42 times. Thereafter, it sharply declined and remained at less than one during 1990-91 to 1993-94. However, since 1994-95 the coverage ratio of the Corporation showed an increasing trend and remained at 30.37 times in 1999-2000. The average coverage ratio of the Corporation was found to be 4.95 times during the study period. It is further marked from the table that during the later part of the study period the EBIT of the Corporation exhibited a rising trend which allowed higher interest coverage for the debt securities. A close look into the coefficient of variation and coefficient of correlation figures reveal that there is a wide variation between EBIT and interest and they also move in opposite direction. On the whole, the Corporation maintained relatively good coverage during the later part of the study period.

Activity Ratios

Activity ratios are concerned with measuring the efficiency of asset management. Funds of creditors and owners are invested in various assets to generate sales and profits. Better management of assets would result in larger amount of sales.

TABLE 5.5
INTEREST COVERAGE RATIO OF THE OSWC

(Rs. in lakh)

Year	*Earning before interest & taxes*	*Interest*	*Interest coverage ratio (Times)*
1985-86	53.11	18.00	2.95
1986-87	65.41	26.26	2.49
1987-88	95.47	27.89	3.42
1988-89	85.33	26.88	3.17
1989-90	52.91	26.68	1.98
1990-91	(-)0.88	27.00	(-)0.03
1991-92	(-)1.67	28.23	(-)0.05
1992-93	5.62	34.65	0.16
1993-94	2.01	36.04	0.05
1994-95	61.83	35.62	1.73
1995-96	104.66	32.50	3.22
1996-97	119.53	25.50	4.68
1997-98	142.82	19.00	7.51
1998-99	140.90	11.17	12.61
1999-2000	115.42	3.80	30.37
Average	69.49	25.28	4.95
S.D.	51.07	9.02	-
C.V.	73.49	35.68	
r	-	-	-0.58

Source: Compiled from the Annual Reports of the OSWC, Bhubaneswar.

Activity ratios, also known as efficiency or asset management or turnover ratios because these ratios indicate the speed with which assets are being converted or turned over into sales. Activity ratios, thus, involve a relationship between sales and assets. A proper balance between sales and assets generally reflects that assets are managed well. The assets communicate the financial facts about an enterpise or economic entity to those who have an interest in interpreting and using those facts. These serve as means for analysing and controlling the operations of the enterprise and for planning future action.[25] Important assets turnover ratios namely, total assets turnover, fixed assets turnover, current assets turnover, working capital turnover and capital turnover of the OSWC are discussed in the following section.

(i) Total Assets Turnover

The total assets turnover ratio shows the firm's ability in generating sales from all financial resources committed to total assets. Total assets include net fixed assets and current assets. The total assets turnover ratio is calculated as follows.

$$\text{Total assets turnover} = \frac{\text{Sales}}{\text{Total assets}}$$

The total assets turnover ratio of the Orissa State Warehousing Corporation for the last 15 years are presented in Table 5.6. The total assets turnover ratio of the OSWC showed a fluctuating trend during the study period. It ranged from 0.27 time in 1993-94 to 0.55 time in 1998-99. A close look into the figures reveals that the ratio values depicted an increasing trend in the early and later part of the study period. The mid-part of the study period revealed an altogether downward trend in the total assets turnover ratio values. The average ratio for the study period was found to be 0.40 time. On the whole, for one rupee of assets the Corporation did not generate even 50 paise of sales except in certain years. From the above analysis, it may be concluded that the total assets turnover of the OSWC is not satisfactory.

(ii) Fixed Assets Turnover

The fixed assets turnover measures the efficiency at which the fixed assets of the firm are used to generate sales. In other words, it is an indicator of the firm's ability in generating sales from its fixed assets. The fixed assets turnover ratio is calculated by dividing the sales by the fixed assets.

$$\text{Fixed assets turnover} = \frac{\text{Sales}}{\text{Fixed assets}} \times 100$$

TABLE 5.6

TOTAL ASSETS TURNOVER RATIO OF THE OSWC

(Rs. in lakh)

Year	*Sales*	*Total assets*	*Total assets turn-over ratio (times)*
1985-86	196.75	675.25	0.29
1986-87	238.82	773.56	0.31
1987-88	360.92	934.01	0.38
1988-89	403.47	1081.02	0.37
1989-90	394.90	1203.48	0.31
1990-91	442.14	1442.97	0.31
1991-92	423.01	1411.26	0.30
1992-93	423.82	1463.51	0.29
1993-94	420.01	1570.25	0.27
1994-95	540.46	1588.34	0.34
1995-96	645.92	1666.30	0.33
1996-97	867.98	1831.09	0.47
1997-98	1133.97	2221.34	0.51
1998-99	1261.04	2278.49	0.55
1999-2000	1347.60	2697.91	0.50
Average	606.72	1522.79	0.40
S.D.	369.20	567.56	—
C.V.	60.85	37.27	—
r	—	—	0.95

Source: Compiled from the Annual Reports of the OSWC, Bhubaneswar.

The fixed assets turnover ratio of the OSWC for the study period is presented in Table 5.7. It is marked from the table that the ratio values depicted a fluctuating trend during 1985-86 to 1992-93. Thereafter, it showed an upward trend till the end of the study period. The ratio values ranged between 0.63 time in 1986-87 to 1.90 times in 1998-99. The Corporation achieved an average fixed assets turnover value of 1.09 during the study period. A close look into the table reveals that the fixed assets turnover value of the OSWC was relatively more in the later part than the early part of the study period. The average value suggests that given a rupee of investment in fixed assets, the Corporation generated Re. 1.09 sales during the study period. On the whole, it may be concluded that the fixed assets turnover of the OSWC was better than the total assets turnover during the study period.

TABLE 5.7
FIXED ASSESTS TURNOVER RATIO OF THE OSWC

(Rs. in lakh)

Year	*Sales*	*Net fixed asset*	*Fixed assets turnover ratio (times)*
1985-86	196.75	305.77	0.64
1986-87	238.82	377.88	0.63
1987-88	360.92	447.80	0.80
1988-89	403.47	514.04	0.78
1989-90	394.90	523.54	0.75
1990-91	442.14	561.19	0.79
1991-92	423.01	577.19	0.73
1992-93	423.82	603.83	0.70
1993-94	420.01	595.20	0.71
1994-95	540.46	579.91	0.93
1995-96	645.92	613.32	1.05
1996-97	867.98	609.10	1.42
1997-98	1133.97	619.30	1.83
1998-99	1261.04	662.51	1.90
1999-2000	1347.60	732.45	1.84
Average	606.72	554.74	1.09
S.D.	369.20	108.99	—
C.V.	60.85	19.64	—
r.	—	—	0.77

Source: Compiled from the Annual Reports of the OSWC, Bhubaneswar.

(iii) Current Assets Turnover

Current assets turnover is the measure of efficiency of a firm in managing and utilizing its current assets. Current assets turnover gives an overall impression as to how frequently the investment in current assets is turned over. The higher the turnover of current assets, the more efficient is the management and utilization of the same while low turnover is an indicative of under utilization of current assets. The current assets turnover is obtained by dividing sales by current assets.

$$\text{Current assets turnover} = \frac{\text{Sales}}{\text{Current assets}}$$

In order to know the efficiency of utilizing current assets, the current assets turnover ratio has been calculated for the Orissa State Warehousing Corporation during the period from 1985-86 to 1999-2000 and presented in Table 5.8.

It is observed from the table that the current assets turnover ratio of the OSWC revealed a fluctuating trend during the study period. A thorough scrutiny of the turnover values reveals that there was increasing trend in the early and later part of the study period. Further, the lowest and highest turnover values were recorded during 1993-94 with 0.43 time and 1998-99 with 0.78 time respectively. However, the Corporation recorded an average current assets turnover of 0.63 time during the said period. It can be concluded that for every rupee of investment in current assets, the Corporation generated Re.0.63 paise sales on an average during the study period. A comparison between fixed assets turnover and current assets turnover suggests that fixed assets were efficiently utilized than the current assets.

TABLE 5.8
CURRENT ASSETS TURNOVER RATIO OF THE OSWC

(Rs. in lakh)

Year	*Sales*	*Current assets*	*Current assets turn-over ratio (times)*
1985-86	196.75	369.47	0.53
1986-87	238.82	395.68	0.60
1987-88	360.92	491.20	0.73
1988-89	403.47	566.97	0.71
1989-90	394.90	679.93	0.58
1990-91	442.14	881.77	0.50
1991-92	423.01	834.07	0.51
1992-93	423.82	859.67	0.49
1993-94	420.01	975.05	0.43
1994-95	540.46	1008.42	0.54
1995-96	645.92	1052.98	0.61
1996-97	867.98	1224.99	0.71
1997-98	1133.97	1602.04	0.71
1998-99	1261.04	1615.97	0.78
1999-2000	1347.60	1965.45	0.69
Average	606.72	968.24	0.63
S.D.	369.21	469.48	—
C.V.	60.85	48.49	—
r.	—	—	0.96

Source: Compiled from the Annual Reports of the OSWC, Bhubaneswar.

(iv) Working Capital Turnover

Working capital of a firm is directly related to its day to day business operations. Inadequacy or mismanagement of working capital is the leading cause of business failures. Therefore, the management of working capital assumes greater significance for the survival and growth of an enterprise.

Working capital turnover indicates the velocity of the utilization of net working capital. This ratio shows the quantum of net working capital utilized to generate a stipulated volume of sales. That is to say, it indicates the efficiency or otherwise in the utilization of short-term funds in making sales. The net working capital turnover ratio can be computed by dividing sales by net working capital.

$$\text{Net working capital turnover ratio} = \frac{\text{Sales}}{\text{Net working capital}} \times 100$$

Table 5.9 presents the net working capital turnover ratio of the Orissa State Warehousing Corporation for the period from 1985-86 to 1999-2000, i.e., for a period of 15 years.

TABLE 5.9

WORKING CAPITAL TURNOVER RATIO OF THE OSWC

(Rs. in lakh)

Year	*Sales*	*Net working capital*	*Working capital tunrover ratio (times)*
1985-86	196.75	150.02	1.31
1986-87	238.82	131.40	1.82
1987-88	360.92	141.81	2.54
1988-89	403.47	92.71	4.35
1989-90	394.90	80.65	4.90
1990-91	442.14	18.46	23.94
1991-92	423.01	(-)26.57	(-)15.92
1992-93	423.82	(-)68.71	(-) 6.17
1993-94	420.01	(-)67.93	(-) 6.18
1994-95	540.46	3.03	177.86
1995-96	645.92	17.03	37.92
1996-97	867.98	78.15	11.10
1997-98	1133.97	179.54	6.31
1998-99	1261.04	195.36	6.45
1999-2000	1347.60	201.16	6.70
Average	606.72	75.07	8.08
S.D.	369.21	91.84	—
C.V.	60.85	122.34	—
r	—	—	0.50

Source: Compiled from the Annual Reports of the OSWC, Bhubaneswar.

This ratio has been expressed in number of times. The net working capital turnover ratio trend during the study period revealed three distinct phases: an initial increasing trend followed by negative trend and declining trend. However, the ratio values fluctuated in between 1.31 times in 1985-86 to 177.86 times in 1994-95. It is marked from the table that the ratio values of later years were found to be higher than the initial years. During 1991-92 to 1993-94, the Orissa State Warehousing Corporation recorded negative turnover values due to the excess of current liabilities over current assets. The average working capital turnover ratio value of the Orissa State Warehousing Corporation stood at 8.08 times during the study period. From the above analysis, it can be concluded that the negative or high working capital turnover witnessed during the mid-study period was due to negative/poor working capital position of the Corporation.

(v) Capital Turnover

Capital turnover ratio is another important turnover ratio which measures the efficiency in the management of capital of a firm. This ratio indicates how efficiently the capital employed in the firm are utilized in generating revenue/sales. Under activity ratio group, this ratio assumes special importance because it is the capital of outsiders and insiders employed in the business to generate revenue. Higher ratio value is the indication that the capital employed is utilized efficiently and vice-versa. The capital turnover ratio is calculated by dividing the sales by the capital employed. Capital employed means the capital supplied by long term creditors and the shareholders. The formula to calculate the capital turnover ratio is as follows.

$$\text{Capital turnover ratio} = \frac{\text{Sales}}{\text{Capital employed}}$$

The Capital turnover ratio of the Orissa State Warehousing Corporation is presented in Table 5.10. It is seen from the table that the ratio values depicted a constant rising trend throughout the study period. It ranged from 0.43 time in 1985-86 to 1.47 times in 1998-99. It is marked from the table that the capital turnover ratio during 1995-96 to 1999-2000 remained at more than 1 time which means that for one rupee capital invested the Corporation generated more than one rupee sales. The Corporation attained an average capital turnover ratio of 0.96 time during the study period.

TABLE 5.10
CAPITAL TURNOVER RATIO OF THE OSWC

(Rs. in lakh)

Year	*Sales*	*Capital employed*	*Capital turnover ratio (times)*
1985-86	196.75	455.80	0.43
1986-87	238.82	509.29	0.47
1987-88	360.92	589.62	0.61
1988-89	403.47	606.75	0.66
1989-90	394.90	604.20	0.65
1990-91	442.14	579.66	0.76
1991-92	423.01	550.62	0.77
1992-93	423.82	535.12	0.79
1993-94	420.01	527.26	0.80
1994-95	540.46	582.95	0.93
1995-96	645.92	630.36	1.02
1996-97	867.98	687.26	1.26
1997-98	1133.97	798.85	1.42
1998-99	1261.04	857.88	1.47
1999-2000	1347.60	933.61	1.44
Average	606.72	629.95	0.96
S.D.	369.21	134.76	—
C.V.	60.85	21.39	—
r	—	—	0.79

Source: Compiled from the Annual Reports of the OSWC, Bhubaneswar.

From the foregoing analysis on assets turnover ratios, it can be concluded that the fixed assets of the Corporation were efficiently utilized as compared to current assets. On the other hand, the current assets of the Corporation grew at a faster rate during the study period but its utilization was not satisfactory. This may be due to the presence of idle stock in the current assets portfolio. Further, it is marked from the coefficient of variation figures of different assets that the coefficient of variation was more in case of working capital than other assets. Similarly, the coefficient of correlation between sales and net working capital is relatively less than the coefficient of correlation between sales and other assets. It can be stated that the working capital management is relatively poor as compared to fixed assets management of the OSWC.

Profitability Ratios

The primary objective of a business undertaking is to earn profit. Profit is the indicator of the financial results of business operations. Profit earning is considered essential for the survival of the business. In the words of Lord Keynes, "Profit is the engine that drives the business enterprises".[26] A business needs profit not only for its existence but also for expansion and diversification. The investors want an adequate return on their investment, workers want higher wages, creditors want higher security for their interest and loan and so on. A business enterprise can discharge its obligation to various segments of the society only through profit. Profit is the difference between revenue and expenditure over a period of time. Profit is a useful measure of overall efficiency of business concern. Profit to the management is the test of efficiency and a measurement of control; to owners, a measure of worth of investment; to the creditors, the margin of safety; to employees, a source of fringe benefits; to the shareholders, a source of reasonable return on their investment, etc. Therefore, profitability ratios are calculated to measure the operating efficiency of the company. There are two major ways by which the profitability of an undertaking can be expressed. They are:

(i) Profitability in relation to sales; and

(ii) Profitability in relation to investment.

Under the first category, the important profitability ratios namely, gross profit margin and net profit margin are selected and examined. In the second category, the ratios namely return on assets, return on capital employed, return on share holders equity etc. are analyzed. A brief analysis on the above mentioned profitability ratios of the OSWC is made in the following paragraphs.

Profit Margin

Profit margin is the return generated by a company's assets and represents the difference between revenues and total expenditure.[27] The profit margin is a measure of overall profitability. This measure is also referred to as the net income percentage or the return on sales.[28] On making an analytical study on the profit margin of a business undertaking, important profit margin ratios like gross profit margin and net profit margin are analysed. A brief analysis on these ratios of the OSWC are outlined below.

Gross Profit Margin

One of the important profitability ratios in relation to sales is the gross profit margin. It indicates the efficiency with which management produces each unit of product. This ratio indicates the average speed between the cost of goods sold and the sales.[29] It expresses the relationship between gross profit on sales to sales in percentage term.

A high ratio is a sign of good management. A gross margin may increase due to the following factors[30]: (i) higher sales prices, cost of goods sold remaining constant, (ii) lower cost of goods sold, sales prices remaining constant, and (iii) a higher sales price with lower cost of goods sold. It is advisable to investigate the factors having a bearing on the high gross margin.

A relatively low gross margin is a danger signal; which needs a detailed examination of factors responsible for it. The important contributory factors are : (i) high cost of production, and (ii) a low selling price resulting from severe competition, inferior quality of products, lack of demand etc. The gross profit margin is calculated by dividing the gross profit by sales.

$$\text{Gross profit margin} = \frac{\text{Sales} - \text{cost of goods sold}}{\text{Sales}} \times 100$$

$$= \frac{\text{Gross profit}}{\text{Sales}} \times 100$$

Table 5.11 presents the gross profit margin ratio of the Orissa State Warehousing Corporation. The gross profit margin ratio is expressed in percentage. During 1985-86 and 1986-87, the gross profit to net sales was about 31 per cent. Thereafter, it steadily declined and remained at 3.5 per cent in 1990-91. Then again it slowly picked up and remained at 19.31 per cent in 1995-96. Finally, it started downward movement and remained at 10.66 per cent in 1999-2000. From the movement of gross profit margin of the OSWC, it is observed that the gross profit margin exhibited three distinct phases such as initial decrease followed by increase and decrease in gross profit margin values. However, the average gross profit margin of the OSWC was found to be 14.37 per cent during the study period. A detail analysis of the table further reveals that the gross profit margin of the OSWC was relatively better during early and later part of the study period.

TABLE 5.11
GROSS PROFIT MARGIN OF THE OSWC

(Rs. in lakh)

Year	*Gross Profit*	*Sales*	*Gross margin ratio (%)*
1985-86	61.67	196.75	31.34
1986-87	75.69	238.82	31.69
1987-88	108.57	360.92	30.08
1988-89	99.20	403.47	24.58
1989-90	67.79	394.90	17.16
1990-91	15.49	442.14	3.50
1991-92	15.84	423.01	3.73
1992-93	24.41	423.82	5.75
1993-94	21.32	420.01	5.07
1994-95	80.67	540.46	14.92
1995-96	124.75	645.92	19.31
1996-97	140.43	867.98	16.17
1997-98	164.31	1133.97	14.48
1998-99	164.36	1,261.04	13.03
1999-2000	143.73	1,347.60	10.66
Average	87.21	606.72	14.37
S.D.	53.22	369.21	—
C.V.	61.03	60.85	—
r	—	—	0.76

Source: Compiled from the Annual Reports of the OSWC, Bhubaneswar.

Net Profit Margin

Net profit margin establishes a relationship between net profit (after taxes) and net sales. The net profit margin is an indicative of management's ability to operate the business with sufficient success not only to recover from revenues of the period, the cost of merchandise or services, the expenses of operating the business (including depreciation) and cost of borrowed funds, but also leave a margin of reasonable compensation to the owners for providing their capital at risk. The ratio of net profit (after interest and taxes) to net sales essentially express the cost-price effectiveness of the operation.[31]

A high net profit margin would ensure adequate return to the owners and enable a firm to withstand adverse economic conditions when the selling price is declining, cost of production is rising and demand for the product is falling.[32] In case the net profit margin is inadequate, the company will not be in a position to pay off its debts and give a satisfactory return to its share holders. The ratio is expressed as follows :

$$\text{Net profit margin} = \frac{\text{Net profit}}{\text{Net sales}} \times 100$$

Table 5.12 shows the net profit as a percentage to net sales of the Orissa State Warehousing Corporation. The ratio values fluctuated from 5.79 per cent in 1988-99 to 17.58 per cent in 1985-86. In 1985-86 the ratio was 17.58 per cent which then fell sharply and became negative till 1993-94. From 1994-95 onwards, the ratio values became positive and showed an upward trend ranging in between 8.25 per cent and 12.56 per cent. The average net profit margin was found to be 7.11 per cent during the study period. A close look into the table reveals that the net margin of the OSWC was relatively better in the early and later part of the study period.

The foregoing analysis on profit margin reveals that the Corporation recorded on an average 14.37 per cent and 7.11 per cent as gross margin and net margin respectively during the study period. The low percentage of net margin is due to rise in the establishment cost on one hand and under-utilization of warehousing facilities on the other hand. Further, it is noticed from the statistical analysis that the coefficient of variation in net profit margin is much higher than the coefficient of variation in gross profit margin. This is due to negative return of the Corporation in certain years.

TABLE 5.12
NET PROFIT MARGIN OF THE OSWC

(Rs. in lakh)

Year	*Net profit*	*Net sales*	*Net margin ratio (%)*
1985-86	34.60	196.75	17.58
1986-87	34.84	238.82	14.58
1987-88	55.04	360.92	15.24
1988-89	23.38	403.47	5.79
1989-90	26.75	394.90	6.62
1990-91	(-)28.49	442.14	(-) 6.44
1991-92	(-)28.28	423.01	(-) 6.68
1992-93	(-)35.82	423.82	(-) 8.45
1993-94	(-)25.77	420.01	(-) 6.13
1994-95	44.64	540.46	8.25
1995-96	63.84	645.92	9.88
1996-97	95.25	867.98	10.97
1997-98	142.49	1133.97	12.56
1998-99	123.32	1261.04	9.77
1999-2000	121.85	1347.60	9.04
Average	43.17	606.72	7.11
S. D.	58.43	369.21	—
C.V.	135.33	60.85	—
r.	—	—	0.79

Source: Compiled from the Annual Reports of the OSWC, Bhubaneswar.

Profitability in Relation to Investment

The second group of profitability ratios express relationship between profit and investment. The most commonly used measure of profitability to investment is to relate the profit output with the capital input and thus to compute the rate of return on capital investment. This rate is the end product of a series of quantitative variables representing different inter-connected and independent factors of business operations.[33] Stated otherwise, the rate of return or Return on Investment (ROI) is equal to the profit margin on sales multiplied by the assets (investment) turnover. There are three different concepts of investments in vogue in financial literature : assets, capital employed and shareholders equity.[34] Based on each of them there are three broad categories of ROIs. They are : (a) return on assets, (b) return on capital employed and (c) return on shareholders' equity. A brief analysis on these three types of investments in relation to the net profit of the OSWC is made in the following paragraphs.

(i) Return on Assets

The Return on Assets (ROA) is an important indicator of profitability in relation to investment. It establishes relationship between net profit with assets of the firm. Stated otherwise, it measures profitability on the investment of a firm. The ROA can be calculated by the following formula.

$$\text{Return on assets} = \frac{\text{Net profit after taxes}}{\text{Total assets}} \times 100$$

Table 5.13 visualises the net profit after taxes as a percentage of the total assets. In the OSWC, the net profit after taxes to total assets had shown fluctuating trend throughout the study period. In the initial three years i.e. 1985-86, 1986-87 and 1987-88, the ratio values were 5.12 per cent, 4.50 per cent and 5.86 per cent respectively. Thereafter, the ratio values decreased to 2.16 per cent in 1988-89 and 2.22 per cent in 1989-90. From 1990-91 to 1993-94, the ROA showed negative values. However, from 1994-95 to 1997-98, the ratio value started rising from 2.81 per cent in 1994-95 and reached to 6.41 per cent during 1997-98. Thereafter, again it declined to 4.52 per cent during 1999-2000. The average ROA of the OSWC was found to be 2.83 per cent during the study period. It can be noted here that the ROA of the OSWC was better in first three years and last four years than the middle years of the study period.

TABLE 5.13
RETURN ON ASSETS OF THE OSWC

(Rs. in lakh)

Year	*Net profit after tax*	*Total assets*	*Ratio (%)*
1985-86	34.60	675.25	5.12
1986-87	34.84	773.56	4.50
1987-88	55.04	939.01	5.86
1988-89	23.38	1081.02	2.16
1989-90	26.75	1203.48	2.22
1990-91	(-)28.49	1442.97	(-)1.97
1991-92	(-)28.28	1411.26	(-)2.00
1992-93	(-)35.82	1463.51	(-)2.42
1993-94	(-)25.77	1570.25	(-)1.64
1994-95	44.64	1588.34	2.81
1995-96	63.84	1666.30	3.83
1996-97	95.25	1834.09	5.19
1997-98	142.49	2221.34	6.41
1998-99	123.32	2278.49	5.41
1999-2000	121.85	2697.91	4.52
Average	43.17	1523.12	2.83
S.D.	58.43	567.19	—
C.V.	135.33	37.24	—
r.	—	—	0.59

Source: Compiled from the Annual Reports of the OSWC, Bhubaneswar.

(ii) Return on Capital Employed

Return on Capital Employed (ROCE) establishes the relationship between profit and capital employed. Return on capital employed is the most widely used ratio to measure the overall profitability and efficiency of a business. The two most widely used concepts are :

(a) Return on gross capital employed; and

(b) Return on net capital employed

(a) Return on Gross Capital Employed

Gross capital employed means funds invested in acquiring the fixed assets and current assets. In order to arrive at the ratio of return on gross capital employed, the net profit before interest and taxes is to be divided by gross capital employed. This ratio is helpful in evaluating the overall profit earning capacity of the business firm. Higher the ratio, the better is the profitability and vice-versa. The formula used to calculate this ratio is as follows.

$$\text{Return on gross capital employed} = \frac{\text{Net profit before interest and taxes}}{\text{Gross capital employed}} \times 100$$

Table 5.14 shows the net profit before interest and taxes as a percentage of gross capital employed of the OSWC. The ratio values showed a fluctuating trend during the study period. In 1985-86, the ratio value was 7.86 per cent and then increased to 10.16 per cent during 1987-88. Thereafter, the ratio values showed a declining trend till 1993-94. However, from 1994-95 to 1996-97, the trend was in increasing order. From 1997-98 to 1999-2000, the ratio registered declining trend and remained at 4.27 per cent in 1999-2000. However, the OSWC recorded an average return on gross capital employed of 4.56 per cent for the study period.

TABLE 5.14
RETURN ON GROSS CAPITAL EMPLOYED OF THE OSWC

(Rs. in lakh)

Year	*Net profit before interest and taxes*	*Gross capital employed*	*Ratio (%)*
1985-86	53.11	675.25	7.86
1986-87	65.41	773.56	8.45
1987-88	95.47	939.01	10.16
1988-89	85.33	1081.02	7.89
1989-90	52.91	1203.48	4.39
1990-91	(-)0.58	1442.97	(-)0.26
1991-92	(-)1.67	1411.26	(-)0.11
1992-93	5.62	1463.51	0.38
1993-94	2.01	1570.25	0.12
1994-95	61.83	1588.34	3.89
1995-96	104.66	1666.30	6.28
1996-97	119.53	1834.09	6.51
1997-98	142.82	2221.34	6.42
1998-99	140.90	2278.49	6.18
1999-2000	115.42	2697.91	4.27
Average	69.51	1523.12	4.56
S.D.	51.04	576.19	—
C.V.	73.43	37.24	—
r.	—	—	0.48

Source: Compiled from the Annual Reports of the OSWC, Bhubaneswar.

From the above analysis, it is marked that the return on gross capital employed was maximum with 10.16 per cent in 1987-88 and minimum with 0.12 per cent during 1993-94. The figures further revealed that during the initial years of the study period the OSWC achieved more return on gross capital employed than the later years. But the return on gross capital employed was negative/marginal during 1990-91 to 1993-94. However, during the rest of the study period, the OSWC recovered and maintained 5 per cent to 7 per cent return on gross capital employed.

(b) Return on Net Capital Employed

The term net capital employed refers to the funds used in acquiring the total assets in a business less its current liabilities. This is another test to judge the overall profitability and efficiency of a business organization. The return on net capital employed can be calculated as below.

$$\text{Return on net capital employed} = \frac{\text{Net profit before interest \& taxes}}{\text{Net capital employed}} \times 100$$

Table 5.15 visualises the net profit before interest and taxes as a percentage of the net capital employed of the Orissa State Warehousing Corporation. The table reveals that the ratio values showed an increasing trend from 11.65 per cent in 1985-86 to 16.19 per cent in 1987-88. Then it reduced to 8.74 per cent in 1989-90 and became negative during 1990-91 and 1991-92. However, the ratio value picked up during 1994-95 and maintained a steady increasing trend till 1997-98. Thereafter, again the ratio value showed a steady downward trend to reach at 12.36 per cent in 1999-2000. The OSWC showed an average ratio value of 11.03 per cent during the study period.

The analysis on return on net capital confirmed that the values exhibited an absolute fluctuating trend throughout the study period. The performance of the OSWC during 1994-95 to 1998-99 was considered satisfactory. In other words, during the said period, the OSWC had efficiently utilized its net capital as compared to rest of the study period.

(iii) Return on Shareholders Equity

In practical sense, the shareholders are the real owners of a business concern. The shareholders assume the highest risk in the business unit. The return on shareholders equity is another important profitability ratio in relation to investment which speaks about the efficiency in the utilization of owners' fund. The shareholders equity or net worth includes paid up share capital, share premium and reserves and surpluses less accumulated losses, if any. The ratio indicates how profitably the owners' funds have been utilized by the firm. A higher ratio reveals that the efficiency in the utilization of owners' fund is satisfactory while a low ratio shows poor profitability and inefficiency in the utilization of owners' fund. The return on shareholder's equity can be calculated as follows.

$$\text{Return on net worth or Shareholder's equity} = \frac{\text{Net profit after interest \& taxes}}{\text{Net woth}} \times 100$$

TABLE 5.15

RETURN ON NET CAPITAL EMPLOYED OF THE OSWC

(Rs. in lakh)

Year	*Net profit before interest & taxes*	*Net capital employed*	*Ratio (%)*
1985-86	53.11	455.80	11.65
1986-87	65.41	509.29	12.84
1987-88	95.47	589.62	16.19
1988-89	85.33	606.75	14.06
1989-90	52.91	604.20	8.74
1990-91	(-)0.58	579.66	(-)0.10
1991-92	(-)1.67	550.62	(-)0.30
1992-93	5.62	535.12	1.05
1993-94	2.01	527.26	0.38
1994-95	61.83	582.95	10.60
1995-96	104.66	630.36	16.60
1996-97	119.53	687.26	17.39
1997-98	142.82	798.85	17.87
1998-99	140.90	857.88	16.42
1999-2000	115.42	933.61	12.36
Average	69.51	629.95	11.03
S.D.	51.04	134.76	—
C.V.	73.43	21.39	—
r	—	—	0.73

Source: Compiled from the Annual Reports of the OSWC, Bhubaneswar.

The return on shareholders' equity of the Orissa State Warehousing Corporation has been exhibited in Table 5.16. In the OSWC, the ratio values fluctuated during the study period, i.e., from (-) 8.36 per cent in 1992-93 to 20.05 per cent in 1997-98. During 1990-91 to 1993-94, the ratio values showed negative figures consecutively for four years. Thereafter, the ratio values became positive and moved up to 20.05 per cent in 1997-98 from 9.36 per cent in 1994-95. Since then, it again declined and remained at 13.23 per cent in 1999-2000. On the whole, the return on shareholders equity during later years are relatively better than the initial years of the study period. Further, the Corporation recorded on an average 8.82 per cent return on net worth during the study period.

TABLE 5.16

RETURN ON SHAREHOLDERS EQUITY OF THE OSWC

(Rs. in lakh)

Year	*Net profit after taxes*	*Net worth*	*Ratio (%)*
1985-86	34.60	237.36	14.57
1986-87	34.84	291.67	11.94
1987-88	55.04	360.42	15.27
1988-89	23.38	389.92	5.99
1989-90	26.75	394.42	6.78
1990-91	(-)28.49	409.86	(-)6.95
1991-92	(-)28.28	419.86	(-)6.73
1992-93	(-)35.82	428.38	(-)8.36
1993-94	(-)25.77	436.90	(-)5.90
1994-95	44.64	476.90	9.36
1995-96	63.84	476.90	13.38
1996-97	95.25	556.90	17.10
1997-98	142.49	710.40	20.05
1998-99	123.32	823.40	14.97
1999-2000	121.85	920.40	13.23
Average	43.17	488.91	8.82
S.D.	58.43	190.27	—
C.V.	135.33	38.92	—
r	—	—	0.71

Source: Compiled from the Annual Reports of the OSWC, Bhubaneswar.

The foregoing analysis on return on investment speaks that the rate of return achieved by the Corporation differs depending upon the selection of variables i.e. profit as well as investment. But one thing is very clear i.e. there is no consistency in the rate of return of the Corporation during the study period.

It is also evident from the statistical analysis that the coefficient of variation in case of profit is much higher than the investment component. It is due to negative earnings witnessed by the OSWC in certain years. Further, the coefficient of correlation between income and investment is positive which means the Corporation is earning profit on its investment.

Apart from the above discussed ratio groups, there is another ratio group known as investibility ratio. Investors while contemplating to invest in shares of a company would be keen to know the investment potentiality of the company before taking final decision. Analysis of investibility ratios helps the investors to know the investibility of the company.[35] In this section, the ratios like Earnings Per Share (EPS), Dividend Per Share (DPS), Pay-out and Du-Pont Return on Investment of the OSWC are analysed.

(iv) Earnings Per Share

The ability of the company to attract more funds from the prospective investors can be measured in a number of ways. One such measure is to calculate the earnings per share (EPS). The earnings per share is calculated by dividing profit after taxes by the total number of equity shares.

$$\text{Earnings per share} = \frac{\text{Profit after taxes}}{\text{Total number of equity shares}}$$

Earnings per share calculated for a number of years indicates whether or not earning power of the firm has increased. As a investibility ratio, the EPS can provide useful information on the basis of its behaviour over a period of time. Accordingly, the investors can take decision to invest their funds in the business concern.

Table 5.17 shows the earnings per share of the Orissa State Warehousing Corporation for the study period. The EPS of the OSWC reflected a fluctuating trend during the study period varying from Rs. 11.35 in 1988-89 to Rs. 47.49 in 1997-98. During 1990-91 to 1993-94 the OSWC's EPS was negative.

TABLE 5.17

EARNINGS PER SHARE OF THE OSWC

(in Rs.)

Year	*Profit after taxes*	*No. of Shares*	*E.P.S.*
1985-86	34,60,332	158960	21.76
1986-87	34,84,803	176960	19.69
1987-88	55,04,835	191960	28.67
1988-89	23,38,859	205960	11.35
1989-90	26,75,482	210960	12.68
1990-91	(-)28,49,082	232960	(-)ve
1991-92	(-)28,28,810	242960	(-)ve
1992-93	(-)35,82,611	251480	(-)ve
1993-94	(-)25,77,715	260000	(-)ve
1994-95	44,64,653	300000	14.88
1995-96	63,84,903	300000	21.28
1996-97	95,25,865	300000	31.75
1997-98	1,42,49,243	300000	47.49
1998-99	1,23,32,292	320000	38.53
1999-2000	1,21,83,076	320000	38.07
Average	43,17,742	251480	17.16
S.D.	5843196	53894.52	—
C.V.	135.32	21.43	—
r	—	—	0.52

Source: Compiled from the Annual Reports of the OSWC, Bhubaneswar.

The EPS values of the OSWC were averaged at Rs.17.16. The EPS of the OSWC especially in later part of the study period is considered satisfactory as compared to early period. The coefficient of correlation between the profit and the number of shares is positive but moderate. In other words, the Corporation is not maintaining the EPS uniformly during the study period. This is mainly due to negative or low income generated in certain years.

Dividend Per Share

As discussed earlier, the net profit after taxes belong to shareholders. The Dividend Per Share (DPS) is the dividend paid to the shareholders on a per share basis. The DPS is a better indicator than EPS, because DPS shows the exact amount received by the shareholders. DPS is calculated by dividing the distributed profit by the number of ordinary shares.

$$\text{Dividend per share} = \frac{\text{Dividend paid to ordinary shareholders}}{\text{No. of shares.}}$$

Table 5.18 shows the dividend per share of the Orissa State Warehousing Corporation during the study period. During 1985-86, the OSWC distributed Rs. 1.75 per share as dividend. The DPS of the OSWC steadily increased to Rs. 5.85 during 1989-90. But thereafter, the Corporation did not declare dividend consecutively for a period of 6 years i.e. from 1990-91 to 1995-96. Again in 1996-97, the Corporation paid Rs. 3.00 as DPS and maintained the same for the rest years of the study period. The average DPS of the Corporation was found to be Rs. 3.81.

TABLE 5.18

DIVIDEND PER SHARE OF THE OSWC

(in Rs.)

Year	*Profit distributed*	*No. of shares*	*DPS*
1985-86	2,78,183	158960	1.75
1986-87	8,57,717	176960	4.89
1987-88	9,41,883	191960	4.90
1988-89	10,03,550	205960	4.87
1989-90	12,34,642	210960	5.85
1990-91	-	232960	-
1991-92	-	242960	-
1992-93	-	251480	-
1993-94	-	260000	-
1994-95	-	300000	-
1995-96	-	300000	-
1996-97	9,00,000	300000	3.00
1997-98	9,25,000	300000	3.08
1998-99	9,60,000	320000	3.00
1999-2000	9,60,000	320000	3.00
Average	5,37,390	251480	3.81

Source: Compiled from the Annual Reports of the OSWC, Bhubaneswar.

Dividend Pay-out Ratio

Dividend payment ratio is also known as pay-out ratio. It is a major factor of dividend policy of a firm. It is an important ratio because ploughing back of profit enables a firm to grow and pay more dividend in future. This explains the percentage of net profit after taxes and preference dividend paid to the equity holders. The dividend pay-out is the ratio of the DPS to EPS.

$$\text{Dividend pay-out ratio} = \frac{\text{Dividend per share}}{\text{Earnings per share}} \times 100 \quad \text{or} \quad \frac{\text{DPS}}{\text{EPS}} \times 100$$

If the DPS ratio is substracted from 100, the balance is the percentage share of the net profit after taxes which is being retained in the business. A higher percentage shows a greater portion of profit being distributed as dividend keeping a small portion of profit as reserves. When percentage is more than 100, it indicates that the past reserves are distributed as dividend to the extent to which it is more than 100%. Like-wise, a lower percentage means keeping more profits as reserves and a negative ratio implies a net loss to the firm.

Table 5.19 shows the DPS as a percentage of EPS of the Orissa State Warehousing Corporation. It is seen from the table that the dividend pay-out ratio of the OSWC during the study period revealed a fluctuating trend ranging from 6.48% in 1997-98 to 46.13% in 1989-90. During 1990-91 to 1995-96, the Corporation did not pay any dividend to its shareholders and hence, the pay-out ratio was nil during the said period. The OSWC had an average dividend pay-out ratio of 14.35%. On the whole, it can be concluded that the OSWC retained more profit during later part of the study period to meet its future expansion programme as compared to the initial years of the study period.

Measurement of Profitability through Du Pont Approach

A measure of profitability is the overall measure of efficiency of a business undertaking. In general terms efficiency in business is measured by the input-output analysis. By measuring the output as a proportion of the input and comparing the results of similar firms or periods, the relative change in its profitability can be established.[36]

The income (output) as compared to the investment (input) indicates the profitability of a firm. Thus, return on investment is one of the most successful yet simple techniques ever conceived to aid both decision making and performance evaluation.

TABLE 5.19
DIVIDEND PAY-OUT RATIO OF THE OSWC

(in Rs.)

Year	*D.P.S.*	*E.P.S.*	*Pay-out (%)*
1985-86	1.75	21.76	8.06
1986-87	4.84	19.69	24.58
1987-88	4.90	28.67	17.09
1988-89	4.87	11.35	42.90
1989-90	5.58	12.68	46.13
1990-91	-	(-)12.22	-
1991-92	-	(-)11.64	-
1992-93	-	(-)14.24	-
1993-94	-	(-) 9.91	-
1994-95	-	14.88	-
1995-96	-	21.28	-
1996-97	3.00	31.75	9.44
1997-98	3.08	47.49	6.48
1998-99	3.00	38.53	7.78
1999-2000	3.00	38.07	7.88
Average	2.28	15.89	14.35

Source: Compiled from the Annual Reports of the OSWC, Bhubaneswar.

Around World War I, the Du Pont Company introduced a method of financial analysis which has general recognition for its usefulness and has, in one form or another been adopted by most firms. Its purpose is to provide management with a measure of performance in the form of a return on investment. It brings together the activity ratios and profit margin on sales and shows how these ratios interact to determine the profitability of assets used in the business. The basic framework of the system is set out in Fig.5.1. In the figure, turnover relates to the effective acquision, utilization and management of assets. The other critical element influencing return on investment is profit margin. This requires an analysis of the structure of the income statement. Thus, Du Pont System of financial control is essentially a framework of financial ratio analysis. The emphasis is on two major aspects in business policy: The effective acquisition and management of assets; and the effective control of costs through analysis of the operating decisions of the firm.[37]

The Du Pont model has been applied to the OSWC to measure the profitability position. The average figures for a period of 15 years i.e. from 1985-86 to 1999-2000 are taken into account to build the Du Pont model. The return on investment through Du Pont model of the OSWC was found to be 2.84% during the study period. The details of profit margin and assets turnover are presented in a decision tree model. Looking at these two aspects, the management can take appropriate steps either to control the cost or improve the assets utilization or both. On the whole, the Du Pont model has in it the greatest strength of presenting the final outcome i.e. the profitability position of the business.

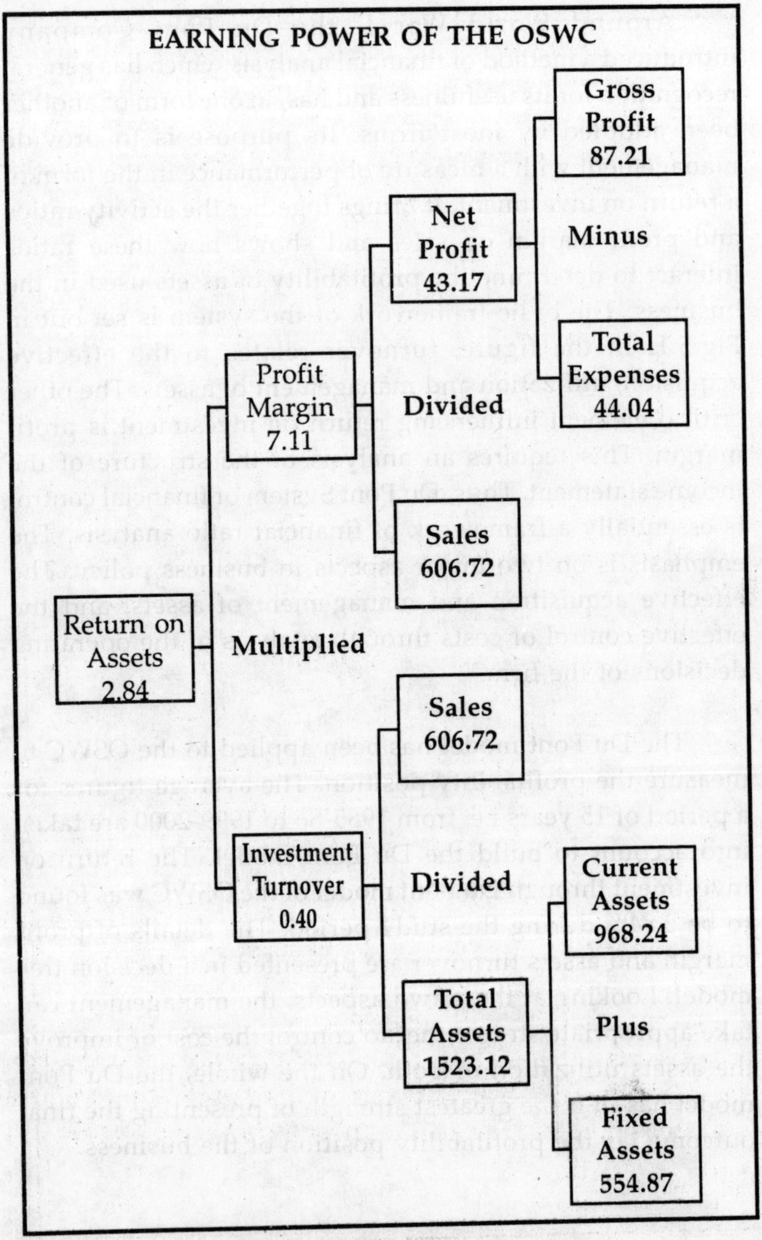

Fig. 5.1: Du Pont Model.

References

1. R.D. Kennedy and S.Y. McMullen, *Financial Statements- Form, Analysis and Interpretation*, Richard D. Irwin Inc., Illinois, 1968, p. 17.
2. J.F. Weston and E.F. Brigham, *Managerial Finance*, Holt, Rinehart and Winston, New York, 1969, p. 67.
3. V.L. Gole, *Fitzgerald's Analysis and Interpretation of Financial Statements*, Butterworths, 1966, p. 2.
4. R.D. Kennedy and S.Y. McMullen, *op. cit.*, p. 17.
5. C.L. Moore, *Managerial Accounting*, Anold Publishers Ltd., London, 1961, p. 119.
6. B. B. Howard and M.Upton, *Introduction to Business Finance*, McGraw Hill Book Company, New York, 1953, p. 61.
7. R.A. Foulke, *Practical Financial Statement Analysis*, McGraw Hill Book Company, New York, 1957, p. 66.
8. *Ibid.*
9. A.S. Dewing, *The Financial Policy of Corporations*, Ronald Press Company, New York, 1953, p. 524.
10. R. N. Anthony, *Management Accounting – Text and Cases*, Richard D. Irwin Inc., Homewood, Illinois, 1964, pp. 293-294.
11. N. L. Hingorani and A. R. Ramanathan, *Management Accounting*, Sultan Chand and Sons, Dellhi, 1973, p. 92.
12. B. Graham and C. McGolrick, *The Interpretation of Financial Statements*, Harper and Row, New York, 1964, p. vii.
13. J. A. Mackinnon and L.J.E. Troupe, *Accounts Analysis*, Gee and Company (Publishers) Ltd., London, 1948, p.1.
14. N.K. Kulshrestha, *Theory and Practice of Management Accounting*, Navman Prakashan, Aligarh, 1976, p. 236.
15. R. N. Anthony, *op. cit*, p. 297.
16. P. Hunt, H. Williams and G. Donaldson, *Basic Business Finance-Text and Cases*, Richand D. Irwin, Illinois, 1966, p. 141.
17. J. Batty, *Management Accounting*, Macdonald and Evans Ltd., London, 1963, p. 374.
18. B. Lev, *Financial Statement Analysis- A New Approach*, Prentice- Hall Inc., Englewood Cliffs, New Jersey, 1974, pp. 36-37.
19. C.F. Lee, *Financial Analysis and Planning- Theory and Application*, Addison- Wesley Publishing Company, U.S.A, 1985, p. 23.
20. *Ibid.*, pp. 23-32.
21. V.S. Kaveri, *Financial Ratios as Predictors of Borrower's Health with Special Reference to Small Scale Industries in India*, Sultan Chand and Sons, New Delhi, 1980, p. 50.

22. J. Batty, *op. cit.*, p. 413.
23. I.M. Pandey, *Financial Management,* Vikas Publishing House Pvt. Ltd., New Delhi, 1994, p. 101.
24. P. Chandra, *Financial Management- Theory and Practice,* Tata McGraw-Hill Publishing Company Ltd., New Delhi, 1984, p. 120.
25. J. Singh and R. Paul, *Management Accounting,* Kitab Mahal, Allahabad, 1982, p. 30.
26. R.K. Sharma and S.K. Gupta, *Management Accounting-Principles and Practice*, Kalyani Publishers, New Delhi, 1983, p. 177.
27. E. Soloman and J. J. Pringle, *An Introduction to Finanacial Management,* Prentice Hall of India Pvt. Ltd., New Delhi, 1978, p. 89.
28. S. C. Kuchhal, *Financial Management- An Analytical and Conceptual Approach,* Chaitanya Publishing House, Allahabad, 1977, p. 71.
29. N. K. Kulshrestha, *Analysis of Financial Statement of Paper Industry in India,* Navman Prakashan, Aligarh, 1972, p. 81.
30. R.N. Anthony and J. S. Reece, *Management Accounting-Principles,* Richard D. Irwin Inc., Illinios, 1975, p. 444.
31. R.D. Kennedy and S.Y. McMullen, *op. cit.,* p.53.
32. M. Y. Khan and P. K. Jain, *Financial Management,* Tata McGraw-Hill Publishing Company Ltd., New Delhi, 1982, p. 139.
33. M.M. Kristen, *Corporation Finance - An Introduction to Principle and Practices,* Harper and Row, New York, 1975, p. 180.
34. M.Y. Khan and P.K. Jain, *op.cit.,* p. 141.
35. R.M. Srivastava, *Financial Management and Policy,* Himalaya Publishing House, New Delhi, 1997, p.67.
36. N.L. Hingorani, A. R. Ramanathan and T.S. Grewal, *Management Accounting,* Sultan Chand & Sons, New Delhi, 1977, p.101.
37. V. K. Bhalla, *Financial Management and Policy*, Anmol Publication Pvt. Ltd., New Delhi, 1998, p. 105.

Six

Analysis of Human Resource Performance of the OSWC

Introduction

The principal resource of an organization is the people. Managing its people is the most important aspect of managing an organization. This is because through the manpower resource only the management essentially wants to direct and control all other resources like materials, machine, money and others. Therefore, it is the most important objective of every management to keep the human power happy and content. In view of this, the importance of Human Resource Management (HRM) in an organization cannot be underestimated. Human Resource Management is a process consisting of four functions-acquisition, development, motivation and maintenance of human resources.[1] Through these functions the objectives of HRM, such as securing industrial peace, high productivity, better quality of working life of employees and obtaining and sustaining competitive advantage through empowerment can be achieved.

An important objective of every organization is survival and growth. The various employees of the organization put their best efforts in order to achieve these objectives. In this regard the HRM ensures that appropriate people, capable of performing effectively the organization's specific tasks, are attracted and secured. Further, they are put to be utilized effectively and generate maximum individual development of the people within the organization.[2] An organization's performance and resulting productivity are directly proportional to the quantity of its human resources.

The human resource aspect of Orissa State Warehousing Corporation is being governed by its "Regulation" named as Orissa State Warehousing Corporation Staff Regulation 1985. The Staff Regulation of the OSWC has been framed in exercise of the powers conferred by section 42 of the Warehousing Corporations Act 1962 (58 of 1962) with the previous sanction of the State Government in Department of Agriculture and Co-operation (Co-operation).[3] On the basis of the contents outlined in the Staff Regulation, the recruitment, promotion and selection of different grades of employees have been made.[4]

In the following pages an attempt has been made to discuss as to whether present work force of the Corporation is sufficient enough to carry out the activities or there is any necessity to add additional work force to the existing number for achieving higher productivity. In order to understand the above aspects the parameters like number of employees, capacity and its utilization, income and expenditure etc. have been taken into consideration.

Employee Strength of the OSWC

The total staff strength of the Corporation as on 31.03.2000 is presented in Table 6.1. The Corporation has employed 483 employees belonging to various categories viz., Class-I, Class-II, Class-III and Class-IV. Out of 483 employees, 120 employees are deployed at the OSWC headquarters at Bhuabenswar and rest 363 employees are working at field level under the administrative control of Zonal Assistant Directors.

TABLE 6.1
ZONE-WISE STAFF STRENGTH OF THE OSWC AS ON MARCH 31, 2000

Name of the zone	*Class I*	*Class II*	*Class III*	*Class IV*	*Total*
Corporate Office	4	15	57	44	120
Balasore	-	1	13	28	42
Bhubaneswar	-	1	11	28	40
Berhampur	-	1	13	27	41
Cuttack	-	2	13	26	41
Titilagrah	-	2	13	25	41
Jagatpur	-	3	16	21	40
Bhawanipatna	-	1	6	17	24
Jeypore	-	1	10	16	27
Rayagada	-	-	10	15	25
Sambalpur	-	3	15	24	42
Total	**4**	**30**	**178**	**271**	**483**

Source: Compiled from the Records of the OSWC, Bhubaneswar.

The staff strength against the sanctioned posts vis-à-vis the percentages of executive and non-executive posts to total staff for a period of 15 years is presented in Table 6.2. It is seen from the said table that the Corporation has never filled up the total sanctioned posts during the study period. The number of executives as a percentage to total number of employees ranged in between 11.72 per cent and 18.64 per cent and like-wise, the percentage figure for non-executives ranged from 81.36 per cent to 88.28 per cent during the study period. It is further marked from the table that the composition of executives and non-executives of the OSWC has tilted in favour of non-executives. From this, it is clear that the Corporation is managing the day to day operations with limited number of executives.

TABLE 6.2
YEAR-WISE BREAK-UP OF STAFF STRENGTH OF THE OSWC

Year	Sanctioned post	Total no. of employees held the post	Executive		Total	Executives as a % to total	Non-executive		Total	Non-executives as a % to total
			Male	Female			Male	Female		
1984-85	342	266	46	-	46	17.30	218	2	220	82.70
1985-86	343	275	46	-	46	16.73	227	2	229	83.27
1986-87	361	266	46	-	46	17.30	217	3	220	82.70
1987-88	362	279	52	-	52	18.64	223	4	227	81.36
1988-89	371	272	43	-	43	15.81	224	5	229	84.19
1989-90	391	305	43	-	43	14.10	256	6	262	85.90
1990-91	392	323	56	-	56	17.34	261	6	267	82.66
1991-92	392	330	53	-	53	16.07	270	7	277	83.93
1992-93	392	332	52	-	52	15.67	272	8	280	84.33
1993-94	392	330	52	-	52	16.07	269	8	277	83.93
1994-95	525	326	48	-	48	14.73	270	8	278	85.27
1995-96	525	498	59	1	60	12.05	425	13	438	87.95
1996-97	525	498	58	1	59	11.85	426	13	439	88.15
1997-98	525	495	57	1	58	11.72	424	13	437	88.28
1998-99	525	485	57	1	58	11.96	414	13	427	88.04
1999-2000	525	483	56	1	57	11.81	412	14	426	88.19

Source: Compiled from the Records of the OSWC, Bhubaneswar.

The employees of the Corporation are categorised under four grades and the same is presented in Table 6.3. From the table, it is noticed that most of the employees belong to Class III and Class IV grade and are coming under the age group of 26-35 and 36-45. With regard to qualification-wise break-up of employees of the OSWC, it is seen from the Table 6.4 that 46 per cent of the total work force are below higher secondary qualification. The graduates and post graduates constitute only 22 per cent of the total work force.

From the above analysis, it can be concluded that the Corporation has deployed more number of Class - IV employees for its day to day transactions particularly in watch and ward duties and so also to assist the Warehouse In-charges, who are coming under either the below higher secondary or higher secondary categories. By deploying such employees in large numbers, the Corporation is not only spending minimum amount towards establishment charges, but also generates savings for the Corporation.

TABLE 6.3
AGE AND GRADE-WISE BREAK-UP OF EMPLOYEES OF THE OSWC

as on March 31, 2000

Grade/Age	*18-25*	*26-35*	*36-45*	*46-58*	*Total*
Class- I	-	-	1	2	3
Class-II	-	-	9	21	30
Class-III	1	30	85	62	178
Class- IV	3	99	129	41	272
Total	**4**	**129**	**224**	**126**	**483**

Source: Compiled from the Records of the OSWC, Bhubaneswar.

TABLE 6.4
QUALIFICATION-WISE BREAK-UP OF EMPLOYEES OF THE OSWC

as on March 31, 2000

Grade	Illiterate	Below higher secondary	Higher secondary	Undergraduate	Graduate	Post-Graduate	Total
Class- I	-	-	2	-	-	1	3
Class-II	-	-	9	4	14	3	30
Class-III	-	6	73	9	78	12	178
Class- IV	-	214	55	3	-	-	272
Total	-	**220**	**139**	**16**	**92**	**16**	**483**

Source: Compiled from the Records of the OSWC, Bhubaneswar.

Income and Expenditure per Employee

Further, in order to know the income / expenditure and profit/loss involved per employee, an analysis has been made for a period of 15 years i.e. from 1985-86 to 1999-2000. The per employee income/expenditure and profit/loss is presented in Table 6.5. The figures in the table indicate that the Corporation had generated surplus funds in shape of profit during the years from 1985-86 to 1989-90 and thereafter incurred losses consecutively from 1990-91 to 1993-94. However, again from 1994-95 to 1999-2000, the Corporation had generated profit.

While going into the year-wise income and expenditure per employee, it is seen that during 1985-86, the per employee profit was Rs. 0.13 lakh but it increased to Rs. 0.25 lakh in 1999-2000. In other words, the Corporation had registered a growth of about 100 percent in profit during the said period.

TABLE 6.5
YEAR-WISE DISTRIBUTION OF INCOME AND EXPENDITURE AND PROFIT AND LOSS PER EMPLOYEE OF THE OSWC

(Rs. in Lakh)

Year	*No. of employees*	*Total income*	*Income per employee*	*Total expen-diture*	*Expendi-ture per employee*	*Net profit/ loss per employee*
1985-86	275	196.76	0.72	162.15	0.59	(+) 0.13
1986-87	266	283.83	0.90	203.98	0.77	(+) 0.13
1987-88	269	360.93	1.34	305.88	1.14	(+) 0.20
1988-89	272	403.47	1.48	280.08	1.40	(+) 0.08
1989-90	305	394.90	1.29	368.15	1.20	(+) 0.09
1990-91	323	442.14	1.37	470.63	1.46	(-) 0.09
1991-92	330	428.02	1.28	451.30	1.37	(-) 0.09
1992-93	332	423.83	1.28	459.65	1.38	(-) 0.10
1993-94	330	420.02	1.27	445.79	1.35	(-) 0.08
1994-95	326	540.46	1.66	495.82	1.52	(+) 0.14
1995-96	498	645.93	1.30	582.08	1.17	(+) 0.13
1996-97	498	867.99	1.74	772.73	1.55	(+) 0.19
1997-98	495	1113.98	2.29	991.48	2.00	(+) 0.29
1998-99	489	1261.04	2.58	1137.72	2.33	(+) 0.25
1999-2000	489	1347.61	2.79	1225.75	2.54	(+) 0.25
Average	**366**	**606.72**	**1.66**	**556.88**	**1.53**	**(+) 0.13**

Source: Compiled from the Records of the OSWC, Bhubaneswar.

Establishment Cost Per Employee

In order to know the expenditure incurred in respect of establishment cost per employee, the same is calculated and presented in Table 6.6. The table shows that the total establishment cost was Rs. 39.39 lakh during 1985-86. However, the same increased to Rs. 337.79 lakh by the end of 1999-2000.

As result, the per employee establishment cost which was Rs. 14,000 during 1985-86 had gone up to Rs. 69,000 during 1999-2000. While looking into the reasons of higher establishment cost over a period of 15 years, it can be stated that the increase in the establishment cost was due to induction of more number of employees during 1989-90, 1990-91 and 1995-96. That apart, the implementation of central pay scale is another contributing factor for such higher expenditures.

TABLE 6.6
YEAR-WISE BREAK-UP OF ESTABLISHMENT COST PER EMPLOYEE OF THE OSWC

(Rs. in Lakh)

Year	*Total no. of employees*	*Total establishment cost*	*Cost per employee*
1985-86	275	39.39	0.14
1986-87	266	49.44	0.18
1987-88	279	54.83	0.19
1988-89	272	66.28	0.24
1989-90	305	75.51	0.24
1990-91	323	90.46	0.28
1991-92	330	106.20	0.38
1992-93	332	116.04	0.34
1993-94	330	127.54	0.38
1994-95	326	138.80	0.42
1995-96	498	181.87	0.36
1996-97	498	242.67	0.48
1997-98	495	303.12	0.61
1998-99	485	335.65	0.69
1999-2000	483	337.79	0.69
Average	**366**	**151.04**	**0.42**

Source: Compiled from the Records of the OSWC, Bhubaneswar.

Establishment Cost per Metric Tonne

The Table 6.7 visualises the expenditure incurred on establishment cost per metric tonne over a period of 15 years. The table reveals that the establishment cost per metric tonne during 1985-86 was only Rs. 28.33 and the same had increased to Rs. 161.62 during 1999-2000 resulting in more than 5 times increase over a period of 15 years. It is further noticed that the average utilization of capacity had a fluctuating trend during the study period and never moved in accordance with the increase of the establishment cost. Therefore, lower capacity utilisation is one of the reasons for hike in establishment cost per metric tonne.

TABLE 6.7

YEAR-WISE BREAK-UP OF ESTABLISHMENT COST PER METRIC TONNE OF THE OSWC

(Rs. in Lakh)

Year	*Total establishment cost*	*Average utilisation in MT (lakh)*	*Establishment cost per MT*
1985-86	39.39	1.39	28.33
1986-87	49.44	1.58	31.29
1987-88	54.83	2.02	27.14
1988-89	66.28	1.64	40.41
1989-90	75.51	1.63	46.32
1990-91	90.46	1.53	59.12
1991-92	106.20	1.63	65.15
1992-93	116.04	1.58	73.44
1993-94	127.54	1.59	80.21
1994-95	138.80	1.42	97.74
1995-96	181.87	1.51	120.44
1996-97	242.67	2.15	112.86
1997-98	303.12	2.19	138.41
1998-99	335.65	2.33	144.05
1999-2000	337.79	2.09	161.62
Average	**151.04**	**1.76**	**85.82**

Source: Compiled from the Records of the OSWC, Bhubaneswar.

Capacity Utilization Per Employee

The capacity utilization per employee during the study period has also been examined and presented in Table 6.8. The table reveals a fluctuating trend with regard to capacity utilisation during the entire study period. In 1985-86, the per employee capacity utilization was 508.38 MT which increased to 745.55 MT during 1987-88. In the later years, it was reduced and finally reached to 434.52 MT during 1999-2000. The declining trend was due to deployment of more number of employees over the years particularly in 1989-90, 1990-91 and 1995-96.

TABLE 6.8

YEAR-WISE BREAK-UP OF CAPACITY UTILIZATION PER EMPLOYEE OF THE OSWC

(in MT)

Year	*Average utilization of capacity*	*Total no. of employees*	*Capacity utilized per employee*
1985-86	139805	275	508.38
1986-87	158672	266	568.71
1987-88	202792	279	745.55
1988-89	164992	272	606.58
1989-90	163286	305	535.36
1990-91	153908	323	476.49
1991-92	163315	330	494.89
1992-93	158857	332	478.48
1993-94	159114	330	482.16
1994-95	142814	326	438.07
1995-96	151429	498	304.07
1996-97	215018	498	431.76
1997-98	219019	495	442.46
1998-99	233136	485	480.69
1999-2000	209876	483	434.52
Average	1,75,735	366	480.16

Source: Compiled from the Records of the OSWC, Bhubaneswar.

The average utilization of capacity per employee during the study period was 480.16 MT. Though the Corporation has increased average utilization to the tune of 0.70 lakh tonne during the study period, the induction of additional 208 employees during the same period resulted in the reduction of average capacity utilization per employee.

Sources of Income Per Employee

As discussed earlier, the OSWC collects storage charges for keeping the commodities in the warehouses. In addition to storage charges, the OSWC also generates some amount of revenue for the services rendered for handling and transportation of stock. In view of this, an attempt has been made to point out whether the storage charges alone can bear the entire burden of the Corporation or not. To examine the problem, the relevant data on storage, handling and transporation charges per employee per annum of the Corporation is presented in Table 6.9. During the early part of the study period, it is observed that, a sizable income of the OSWC was derived from storage charges only, which ranged from 53 per cent to 68 per cent of the total income. However in the later part of the study period the handling and transportation charges contributed significantly and remained within the range of 51 per cent to 57 per cent of the total income of the Corporation. The average income from storage as well as handling and transportation charges was 49.62 per cent and 50.39 per cent respectively during the study period.

From the above analysis, it is seen that income from storage charges alone cannot bear the entire burden of the organization for which ancillary activities like handling and transporation of goods are of vital importance for maintaining the work force deployed by the corporation.

TABLE 6.9
YEAR-WISE DISTRIBUTION OF INCOME FROM STORAGE, HANDLING AND TRANSPORTATION CHARGES PER EMPLOYEE OF THE OSWC

(in Rs.)

Year	*Storage charges*	*Handling & transportation charges*	*Total income per employee*
1985-86	47,245 (66)	24,302 (34)	71,547 (100)
1986-87	53,306 (60)	36,478 (40)	89,784 (100)
1987-88	87,819 (68)	41,545 (32)	1,29,364 (100)
1988-89	78,877 (53)	69,457 (47)	1,48,334 (100)
1989-90	62,182 (48)	67,279 (52)	1,29,479 (100)
1990-91	59,225 (43)	77,661 (57)	1,36,886 (100)
1991-92	59,396 (46)	68,791 (54)	1,28,187 (100)
1992-93	65,110 (51)	62,549 (49)	1,27,659 (100)
1993-94	69,798 (55)	57,480 (45)	1,27,278 (100)
1994-95	82,250 (49)	83,536 (51)	1,65,786 (100)
1995-96	60,906 (47)	68,799 (53)	1,29,705 (100)
1996-97	80,544 (46)	93,751 (54)	1,74,295 (100)
1997-98	1,08,423 (47)	1,20,663 (53)	2,29,086 (100)
1998-99	1,18,970 (46)	1,41,039 (54)	2,60,009 (100)
1999-2000	1,20,212 (43)	1,58,796 (57)	2,79,008 (100)
Average	76,950 (49.62)	78,143 (50.39)	1,55,093 (100)

Figures in parentheses denote percentage to total.
Source: Compiled from the Records of the OSWC, Bhubaneswar.

Assessment on Reorganisation of Staff Strength in Different Zones

As a part of the on going policy for down-sizing the staff strength of the public sector udertakings in Orissa, an analysis has been made for the OSWC to know whether the existing work force is sufficient to carry out the job or there is overstaffing or understaffing in the organisation.

In order to find out the same the zone-wise ratio of manpower and capacity of warehouses are of considerable importance. The study conducted by Social Enrichment Workers' Association (SEWA) in its project report submitted to the OSWC[5] concluded that 60 per cent of the employees are of the opinion that there is no necessity of additional requirement of employees. However, 29 per cent of employees expressed the need for some additional staff for the corporate office and zonal offices.

The study made by SEWA further evaluated the division-wise ratio of manpower and capacity of warehouses and accordingly, developed a standard or quotient. When divided the total capacity by the total manpower of the warehouses the result provides a constant (K). This factor (K) shows the average performance of an employee to manage a specific quantum of storage which is derived as below.

$$\frac{\text{Total capacity}}{\text{Total manpower}} = K$$

Now when the capacity of each zonal warehouses is divided by the factor (K), this would give the result with regard to the required manpower of the various zonal warehouses. In other words, this would reveal whether a particular warehouse has either more or less manpower than the requirement.

$$\frac{\text{Capacity of the Zonal Warehouses}}{K} = \text{Required Manpower}$$

The data with regard to the requirement of manpower and redeployment of manpower in various zones of the OSWC is calculated and presented in Table 6.10. It is noticed from the table that five zones, viz., Balasore, Berhampur, Cuttack, Jeypore and Rayagada have excess manpower than the requirement.

TABLE 6.10
ZONE-WISE REQUIREMENT AND REDEPLOYMENT OF MANPOWER OF THE OSWC AS ON MARCH 31, 2000

Name of the zone	*Total capacity in MT*	*Existing no. of manpower*	*Required no. of manpower*	*Varience*	*% of varience*
Balasore	22885	42	34	8*	(+)19.04
Bhubaneswar	28495	40	42	2**	(–) 5.00
Berhampur	19930	41	29	12*	(+)29.26
Cuttack	16620	41	24	17*	(+)41.46
Titilagarh	35599	41	52	11**	(–)26.82
Jagatpur	29500	40	43	3**	(–)07.50
Bhawanipatna	28681	24	42	18**	(+)75.50
Jeypore	16950	27	25	02*	(+)07.40
Rayagada	12910	25	20	05*	(+)20.00
Sambalpur	35090	42	52	10**	(–)23.80
Total	**2,46,660**	**363**	**363**		

* refers to Surplus
** refers to Deficit
Source: Compiled from the Records of the OSWC, Bhubaneswar.

On the other hand, there is a requirement of additional manpower at Bhubaneswar, Titilagarh, Jagatpur, Bhawanipatna and Sambalpur zones as revealed by the K-factor analysis. So far as work-load per individual employee is concerned, it is extremely high in Bhawanipatna and Titilagarh zones as compared to other zones. In Cuttack and Berhampur zones, there are excess staff to the extent of 17 and 12 respectively than the required numbers as revealed in the table. Further, It is seen that Bhawanipatna and Titlagarh have more shortage of staff to the extent of 18 and 11 respectively. Therefore, a rational distribution of staff in each-zone is required to remove the under and over utilization of staff, and maintain an equilibrium in staffing at different work places.

References

1. N.G. Nair and L. Nair, *Personnel Management and Industrial Relations,* S. Chand and Co. Ltd., New Delhi, 2001, p. 5.
2. B. Ghosh, *Personnel Management and Industrial Relations,* World Press, Calcutta, 1993, p. 25.
3. *The Warehousing Corporations Act, 1962* (58 of 1962), p. 27.
4. *OSWC Staff Regulation,* Notification, The 10th July 1985, *The Orissa Gazettee,* August 30, 1985, pp. 1073-1076.
5. *Manpower Assessment in the OSWC,* A Project Report Submitted to the OSWC by Social Enrichment Workers' Association, Bhubaneswar, 2000, p. 46.

Seven

Summary of the Findings and Suggestions

The present research work on the topic "A Critical Study on the working of the OSWC" has been broadly divided into two parts. The first part deals with the warehousing business in India including its origin, growth and development and the role played by the Warehousing Corporations in the Indian economy. Further, the review of theoretical literature on warehousing activities in India is also included in this part. The second part deals with the empirical analysis on the working of the OSWC. Analysis on three important aspects of the OSWC viz., physical, financial and human resource have been carried out. The tools namely percentage, CAGR, trend analysis, coefficient of variation, coefficient of correlation have been applied in the physical analysis. In the financial analysis portion, the techniques like ratio analysis, trend analysis, percentage, correlation coefficient have been used. In the human resource section, analysis has been made by applying the percentage, trend analysis and K-factor technique. Major findings of both the parts have been summarised and presented in the following paragraphs. Further, important suggestions have also been forwarded to improve the efficiency and productivity of the OSWC.

Warehousing Business in India

Warehousing is a trade which involves the deposit of goods/commodities (under provisions of the Warehousing

Corporations Act, 1962) and wares in the warehouses for the safe custody and its return on payment of storage charges. Warehousing is a specialized economic activity. Warehousing does not mean only preservation of foodgrains. It also provides the facilities and services, incidental or connected with storage, transport, handling and distribution of inputs, products and various other commodities. Thus, warehousing acts as a real and positive contributor to the value of the product.

There is no clear-cut information on the origin of warehousing but the study on fossils of paddy seeds, radio carbon dating etc. reveal that the practice of storing of foodgrains was prevalent since 4500 B.C. The history claims that the preservation of foodgrains was prevalent in ancient times in various parts of the globe. The available records also reveal that in India too the system of storage was practised during 1500 to 500 B.C. The warehousing business on state-run basis in India was evolved on the basis of the recommendation given by various committees constituted to look after the problems faced by the rural mass. In order to mitigate the problem of marketing of agricultural produce in rural areas, the Royal Commission (1928) recommended the establishment of licensed warehouses to preserve the agricultural and allied produce. The All India Rural Credit Survey Committee set-up by the Reserve Bank of India in 1954, reiterated the point already made by the Royal Commission on Agriculture (1928) for the establishment of public warehousing system in India. This Committee's recommendation resulted in the enactment of the Agricultural Produce (Development and Warehousing) Corporations Act, 1956. It was replaced by a more comprehensive Warehousing Corporations Act, 1962.

The objectives of Public Warehousing Corporations are : (a) creation of negotiable paper to provide an instrument for expansion of credit through Commercial Banks for the benefit of the producers, depositors and others, (b) addition to the nation's real income by reducing waste and losses in storage by promoting and developing warehousing system on scientific manner, (c) providing assistance in orderly marketing of agricultural and allied produce through introduction of standard grade specification and (d) assisting Government and Government sponsored organizations to arrive at their schemes on price support and price control.

At present three main agencies in the public sector are engaged themselves in building large-scale godowns/ warehouses. They are Food Corporation of India (FCI), Central Warehousing Corporation (CWC) and 16 State Warehousing Corporations (SWCs). The FCI and the CWC are creating storage facilities at centers of all India importance and SWCs are creating warehousing infrastructures at centers of state/ district level importance. Among these public enterprises, FCI procures foodgrains from the farmers, while the Warehousing Corporations both Central and State, store the produce of the persons who desire so on paying storage charges. The Warehousing Corporation issues a warehouse receipt to the depositor of goods and the same can be pledged with the bank for availing loan.

The data on foodgrains production reveals that during the last decade it has grown at an annual compound rate of 2.65 per cent. Assuming the foodgrains production to grow at the same rate, the production by the end of 2005 would be 2526.77 lakh MT. With the existing storage capacity, only 25 per cent of the total foodgrains can be accommodated thus leaving a wide gap between demand and supply of warehousing facilities. From this, it is inferred that there is a growing need for warehousing facilities in the country to accommodate huge agricultural and allied produce.

Performance of CWC

The Central Warehousing Corporation having a total storage capacity of 74.79 lakh MT is operating with 451 warehouses covering 224 districts of the country. The CWC is the premier organization in providing storage facilities for agricultural produce and allied items. It has vast storage facilities in regions like Hyderabad, Lucknow, Mumbai etc. So far as its utilization of capacity is concerned, it can be stated that due to acceptance of higher level of foodgrains in its warehouses followed by fertilizer, the occupancy position of the CWC was 77 per cent during 1999-2000. It is also observed that the CWC has never been able to utilize its capacity fully during the years of the study period. Even though the capacity is not utilized fully, the CWC is regularly making profit. The main source of revenue of the CWC is warehousing charges and commission from incidental activities. The CWC also discharges promotional activities like FESS and DESS which has contributed significantly to the national economy.

Performance of State Warehousing Corporations

As per the provisions of the Warehousing Corporations Act, 16 states have established their own Warehousing Corporation. Most of these SWCs were established during late fifties. The share capital of the SWCs were equally contributed by the CWC and the concerned State Government. The area of operation of the SWC is confined within the concerned State.

The total number of warehouses of the 16 SWCs is 1440 having a total capacity of 123.74 MTs as on 31.3.2000. On the whole 84.50 per cent of the total capacity was utilized by the SWCs as on the same date. The Karnataka, Meghalaya and Uttar Pradesh SWCs have utilized more than the total capacity, while the Warehousing Corporations of Kerala, Rajasthan,

Haryana and West Bengal utilized only two-third of the total capacity. The major customers of the SWCs are Government Departments, Public Sector Undertakings, Traders, Cooperatives, Small and Marginal farmers. The major commodities accepted for storage are foodgrains, fertilizer, oil seeds, pulses and other notified commodities.

As far as financial performance of the SWCs is concerned, it is noticed that SWCs of Punjab, Haryana, Maharashtra and Uttar Pradesh have generated substantial profit during 1999-2000. The financial performance of the OSWC is considered moderate when compared to average performance of the SWCs taken together.

Prospects and Challenges before Public Sector Warehousing

India has tremendously increased her food production through different plan periods for attaining self-sufficiency. The annual foodgrains production has increased more than four times since 1951-52 crossing the mark of 209 million tons during 1999-2000. Likewise, the demand for fertilizer, pesticides has gone up. Hence, demand for warehousing facilities to accommodate these inputs is growing at a faster rate year after year.

Our past experience has shown that adverse climatic conditions have always made a set back in foodgrains production. Since warehousing business is directly linked with production, vagaries of weather always severely affect the warehousing business prospect. Till recently, warehousing business was owned and managed by public sectors. However, with the announcement of National Storage Policy by the Government of India, considerable amount of incentives can be made available to the private entrepreneurs for setting up of warehouses. The entry of private sectors into warehousing business will certainly affect the monopoly of public sector warehousing undertakings. Therefore, the public warehousing organisation should evolve appropriate business strategy to meet the challenges.

Brief Profile of the OSWC

The Orissa State Warehousing Corporation was set up in the year 1958 by the State Government in complying with the provisions of Warehousing Corporations Act. Initially the Corporation had only two godowns with 860 MT capacity. However, the number of warehouses had gone up to 63 with a total capacity of 2,46,660 MT covering 27 districts as on 31st March,2000. The objectives of the OSWC are to provide institutional credit to the needy farmers, and to minimize storage losses of foodgrains and other agricultural produce by constructing scientific godowns throughout the state. The main commodities, which are accepted for storage in warehouses of the OSWC are foodgrains and fertilizer mostly from Food Corporation of India and fertilizer companies.

Management Structure of the OSWC

The management of the affairs of the OSWC is vested in a Board comprising of 10 Directors. Five Directors are nominated by the CWC and the other five Directors by the State Government. The Chairman and Managing Director are appointed by the State Government. The Managing Director exercises powers and performs such duties as entrusted or delegated by the Board of the OSWC. Apart from a Board, there is an Executive Committee of the OSWC. The Board as well as the Executive Committee have been entrusted to manage the affairs of the Corporation. In a nut shell, the top management of the Corporation vests in (i) the Board of

Directors (ii) the Chairman and (iii) the Managing Director. The Officers of the Corporation have distinct functions who work in close collaboration and coordination for attaining the objectives of the Corporation.

Capital Structure

The share capital of the Corporation at the time of inception was Rs.10 lakh contributed on 50:50 basis both by the CWC and the Orissa State Government. Thereafter, the share capital of the Corporation has been increasing from time to time and at present the share capital stands at Rs. 320 lakh. The total assets of the Corporation are Rs. 2697.91 lakh. However, the long-term loan position of the OSWC is nil during 1999-2000.

Role of the OSWC in the Economy of Orissa

The rural economy of the State is dependent mainly on the agriculture and allied activities. It is estimated that 70 per cent of foodgrains remain with producers for consumption. During the post-harvest period about 6.58 per cent of the foodgrains are spoiled due to defective storage practices at farm level. The OSWC by providing scientific storage in its warehouses controls the wastages and saves wealth of the nation in general and Orissa in particular. Due to presence of godown facilities all over the State the farmers are not compelled to sell their produce immediately after the harvesting of crops. It, therefore, enhances the bargaining power of the farmers and save them from distress sale. On the basis of godown receipts issued against the produce stored in the godowns, the farmers are getting credit from commercial banks easily at reasonable rate. Thus, the warehousing facilities not only minimise wastages but also enable the farmers to get cheap institutional credit and support price for their produce.

The OSWC has associated itself in smooth distribution of essential commodities in the State by eliminating black marketers from public distribution system. That apart, during natural calamities the OSWC is extending its help for easy availability of commodities in the affected areas. The OSWC has also provided direct and indirect employment opportunities to the people of the state in its day-to-day transactions.

Analysis of Physical Performance of the OSWC

The physical performance of the OSWC depends on various factors like, (i) location of godowns, (ii) capacity of godowns, (iii) utilization of space, (iv) condition of godowns, (v) management of storage space, (vi) quality of services and (vii) inspection and physical verification of warehouses, cleanliness etc.

The physical performance of the OSWC has been analyzed taking into account the capacity and occupancy of the warehouses for a period of 15 years, i.e., from 1985-86 to 1999-2000. Further, a detailed analysis on zone-wise, district-wise, month-wise, depositor-wise and commodity-wise has been made. The OSWC had only 47 warehouses having a total average capacity of 1,25,924 MT in 1985-86. Out of the total capacity the percentages of owned capacity and hired capacity were 55.35 per cent and 44.65 per cent respectively. The number of warehouses had gone up to 63 with a total capacity of 2,40,660 MT as on 31st March, 2000. The study reveals that though the capacity has increased over the years, yet the year to year comparison of capacity with utilization reveals a low rate of growth in occupancy. The reason for low capacity utilization is due to opening of very small capacity godowns in the villages under PDS and low quantity of deposit of customs from the depositors of the OSWC.

Month-wise Utilization of Storage Space

The utilization of godown space largely depends on deposits of fertilizer stock as well as procurement of foodgrains in the State. The utilization of godown space is seasonal. It is observed from the study that the peak period for utilization of godowns is normally from January to March followed by a moderate utilization period from April to September. The lean period remains from October to December.

Zone-wise Distribution of Capacity and Occupancy

The zone-wise utilization of capacities reveals that Jagatpur, Titilagarh and Bhawanipatna zones utilized their capacities fully, while under-utilization of warehousing facility was marked in Cuttack, Berhampur and Jeypore zones. The highest and lowest occupancy were marked in Jagatpur and Cuttack zones respectively.

District-wise Distribution of Capacity and Occupancy

The district-wise distribution of capacity and its occupancy showed that the Cuttack, Kendrapara, Balasore, Bhadrak, Gajapati, Sambalpur, Bolangir, Kalahandi and Malkangiri districts handled more stocks than the available warehousing facilities. The highest percentage of utilization of warehouse was marked in Kendrapara district and the lowest was noticed in Boudh and Kandhamal districts.

Category-wise Warehouses and Utilization

The godowns of the OSWC are categorized under four heads namely, 'A', 'B', 'C' and 'D' on the basis of the capacity of the godowns. The 'A' category warehouse has the capacity of 10,000 MT and above. The capacity of 'B', 'C' and 'D' categories of warehouses are in the range of 5,000 MT to 9,999 MT, 1,000 MT to 4,999 MT and below 1000 MT respectively. The 'A' and 'B' category warehouses cover the major portion of total capacity, which is 76.91 per cent of the total capacity. The utilization of space of these warehouses was cent percent. The 'C' category godowns utilized about 59 per cent of the total capacity and likewise, 'D' category godowns utilized about 51 per cent of the total capacity during 1999-2000.

Depositor-wise Utilization

The Depositor-wise utilization of warehouses during study period shows that 41.05 per cent of space has been utilized by Food Corporation of India, followed by 34.64 per cent by fertilizer Companies and 17.60 per cent by State Government departments/organizations. The remaining part has been utilized by cooperatives, traders and farmers.

Commodity-wise Utilization

The commodity-wise utilization of space during the study period revealed that godowns of the OSWC were occupied mainly by foodgrains and fertilizer. The utilization of foodgrains, on an average, was 59.63 per cent followed by fertilizer with 34.64 per cent. Other commodities taken together contributed only 5.73 per cent of the space utilisation during the study period.

Analysis of Financial Performance of the OSWC

Financial statements contain a lot of information. If they are properly analysed and interpreted, the statement can provide valuable insights into a firm's operational and financial performance. Analysis of financial statements is of immense help to several groups interested in a business organisation.

The various interested groups are creditors (both short-term as well as long-term), investors, governments, employees, management, trade association, labour bureau, research institutions, stock exchanges etc. Financial analysis is done for a variety of purposes ranging from a simple analysis of a short-term liquidity position of a firm to a comprehensive assessment of the strengths and weaknesses of the various functional areas. It is done to assess corporate excellence, credit-worthiness, etc. of a firm.

Techniques of Financial Statement Analysis

To analyze the financial statements a number of tools and techniques are available with the analysts. The important among them are (i) comparative statement analysis, (ii) trend analysis, (iii) common-size statement analysis, (iv) funds-flow analysis, (v) cash-flow analysis and (vi) ratio analysis. Statistical techniques like standard deviation, correlation, regression, analysis of time series and analysis of index number etc. are also used alongwith the financial techniques to provide more scientific analysis. In our study only ratio analysis technique is used to analyse the financial statements of the OSWC.

Ratio Analysis

The ratio analysis is one of the most powerful tools of financial analysis. It is an arithmetical relationship between two figures. It is found by dividing one number, the base into the other. Ratios can be expressed in any of the three forms: (i) a pure ratio, e.g. 2:1, (ii) as a rate i.e. in times and (iii) as a percentage. The ratio analysis provides clues especially in identifying trends towards better or poor performance and in finding out significant deviation from the average or relatively applicable standard. Financial ratio is analysed in two ways: (i) time series analysis and (ii) cross-section analysis. The objective of time series analysis is to evaluate the trend of a ratio(s) whereas the cross-section analysis points out any deviation in the representative ratio value by comparing it with the standard.

Classification of Ratios

The use of ratio analysis is not confined to finance manager only. There are different parties interested in the ratio analysis to know the operational and financial position of a firm. In view of various users of ratios, there are many types of ratios, which can be calculated from the information given in the financial statements. However, ratios may broadly be classified on the basis of its source i.e. balance sheet ratios and income statement ratios or on the basis of indication i.e. liquidity, profitability, financial stability and turnover relationship. The later method of classification of ratios is considered significant because it speaks distinctly the different aspects of business activities. The financial performance of the OSWC with regard to its liquidity, profitability and solvency etc. are presented below.

Liquidity

Liquidity refers to the ability of the firm to meet its obligations in short run, usually one year. Liquidity ratios are generally based on the relationship between current assets and current liabilities. The important liquidity ratios are : current ratio and acid test ratio.

Current Ratio

The current ratio of the OSWC in 1985-86 was 1.7:1 which then declined to 0.9:1 in 1993-94. Thereafter, it increased marginally and remained above 1:1 during rest of the study period. It is further noticed that the current ratio of the OSWC was higher in the early part as compared to the rest of the study period. The fall in the current ratio in the later years was due to more increase in current liabilities than the current assets.

Acid Test Ratio

The acid test ratio of the Corporation was 1.7:1 in 1985-86 and then it declined and remained at 0.9:1 in 1993-94. Thereafter, marginal increase was noticed during the rest of the study period. However, the quick ratio of the Corporation during entire study period remained more or less at 1:1. It can be stated that the liquidity position of the OSWC was satisfactory during the study period.

Solvency/Leverage

The leverage refers to the use of debt finance. Two types of ratios are commonly used to analyze leverage : (i) structural ratios and (ii) coverage ratios. Structural ratios are based on the proportions of debt and equity in the financial structure of the firm. Coverage ratios reflect the relationship between debt servicing commitments and sources for meeting these commitments.

Debt-equity Ratio

The debt-equity ratio of the Corporation displayed a downward movement during the study period. The ratio was 1.36:1 in 1985-86 and then reduced and remained at 0.10:1 in 1998-99. The use of low amount of borrowed capital especially during later part of the study period deprived the leverage benefit to the Corporation.

Total Debt Ratio

The Corporation witnessed a continuous rise in quantum of debt proportion, i.e., from 0.48:1 in 1985-86 to 0.70:1 in 1993-94. Thereafter, marginal decline in debt amount was noticed. It is also noticed that the Corporation used more debt finance in the latter part of the study period. However, the rise in debt was mainly due to use of short-term borrowings.

Interest Coverage Ratio

The interest coverage ratio of the Corporation during the years from 1985-86 to 1989-90 were in between 1.98 times and 3.42 times, and then declined sharply and remained at less than one during the years from 1990-91 to 1993-94. However, from 1994-95 the coverage ratio showed an increasing trend and remained at 30.37 times in 1999-2000. It is also marked that the EBIT of the OSWC showed a rising trend which allowed higher interest coverage for the debt securities.

Activity

The activity ratios, also referred as turnover ratios, measure how efficiently the assets are being utilised. These ratios are based on the relationship between the level of activity and the level of various assets. The important activity ratios included in this study are : (i) total assets turnover, (ii) fixed assets turnover, (iii) current assets turnover, (iv) working capital turnover and (v) capital turnover.

Total Assets Turnover

The total assets turnover ratio values of the OSWC depicted an increasing trend in the early as well as in the later part of the study period. The mid-part of the study period revealed a downward trend in the total assets turnover values. It is further noticed that the Corporation achieved total assets turnover value of 0.40, on an average, during the study period. In other words, the Corporation only generated 0.40 paise sales on each rupee of total assets.

Fixed Assets Turnover

The fixed assets turnover ratio values showed a fluctuating trend during early part of the study period and thereafter depicted an upward trend till the end of the study period. It is observed from the study that the fixed assets turnover value was relatively more in the later part than the early part of the study period. On the whole, the Corporation witnessed an average fixed assets turnover value of 1.09 time during the study period. This speaks that given one rupee of fixed assets, the Corporation generated Re.1.09 paise sales.

Current Assets Turnover

The current assets turnover ratio of the OSWC showed a fluctuating trend during the study period. A close scrutiny of the values revealed that there was an increasing trend in the early as well as in the later part of the study period. However, the Corporation achieved an average current assets turnover value of 0.63 time during the study period. It can be stated that for every rupee of investment in current assets the Corporation generated Re. 0.63 paise sales on an average. A comparison between the utilisation of current assets and fixed assets reveals that the fixed assets were efficiently utilized than the current assets.

Working Capital Turnover

It is found out that the net working capital turnover of the OSWC revealed three distinct phases: (i) an initial increasing trend, (ii) negative trend and, (iii) declining trend. The ratio values fluctuated in between 1.31 times in 1985-86 and 177.86 times in 1994-95. During 1991-92 to 1993-94, the Corporation recorded negative turnover. This was due to the poor working capital management by the Corporation.

Capital Turnover

It is noticed that the capital turnover values of the OSWC revealed a constant rising trend. The capital turnover value was 0.43 time in 1985-86 which increased to 1.47 time in 1998-99. On an average, the Corporation achieved capital turnover value of 0.96 time during the study period. From the turnover ratios, it is observed that the fixed assets of the OSWC were efficiently utilized as compared to other category of assets.

Profitability

Profitability ratios are another important category of ratios which portray the final result of business operations. There are two types of profitability ratios. They are : (i) profitability in relation to sales and, (ii) profitability in relation to investment. In the first category the gross profit margin and net profit margin are examined while in the second category, the ratios like return on assets, return on capital employed and return on shareholders equity are studied.

Gross Profit Margin

The gross profit margin of the OSWC was about 31% during 1985-86 to 1986-87. Then it steadily declined and remained at 3.5 per cent in 1990-91. Again, it slowly went up and remained at 19.31 per cent in 1995-96. Ultimately, it started downward movement and remained at 10.66 per cent in 1999-2000. On the whole, the gross profit margin showed three distinct phases, such as initial decrease in gross margin followed by increase and decrease. However, the Corporation attained 14.37 per cent gross margin during the study period.

Net Profit Margin

It is observed that the net profit margin of the OSWC was relatively better in the early as well as in the later part of the study period. The net profit margin during the mid-study period was either negative or minimal. The reasons for such state of affairs in the mid-study period are under utilisation of warehousing facilities and rise in the establishment cost of the Corporation.

Return on Assets

It is found out from the study that the return on assets revealed a fluctuating trend throughout the study period. The return on assets of the OSWC was relatively better during the first three years and also the last four years than the middle years of the study period. The Corporation, on an average, attained 2.83 per cent return on assets during the study period.

Return on Gross Capital Employed

The return on gross capital employed values of the OSWC showed a fluctuating trend during the study period. The average return on gross capital employed of the OSWC during the study period was 4.56 per cent. It is marked from the study that the return on gross capital employed was maximum with 10.16 per cent in 1987-88 and minimum with 0.12 per cent in 1993-94.

Return on Net Capital Employed

The return on net capital employed values depicted an absolute fluctuating trend throughout the study period. It ranged from 0.38 per cent in 1993-94 to 17.87 per cent in 1997-98 excluding the negative values. The Corporation achieved, on an average, 11.03 per cent return on net capital employed during the study period. On the whole, the performance of the Corporation in terms of return on net capital employed was satisfactory during later part as compared to early part of the study period.

Return on Shareholders Equity

The rate of return on net worth of the OSWC during later years are relatively better than the initial years of the study period. The OSWC witnessed on an average 8.82 per cent return on net worth during the study period. Further, the return on net worth was negative during the period from 1990-91 to 1993-94 because the Corporation sustained losses during the said period.

Earnings per Share

The EPS of the OSWC reflected a fluctuating trend varying from Rs. 11.35 in 1988-89 to Rs. 47.49 in 1997-98. The EPS was negative during 1990-91 to 1993-94. The EPS of the OSWC in later part of the study period was considered satisfactory than the early period. The EPS value shows that the OSWC could not maintain consistency in EPS value. This is due to low income generated in certain years.

Dividend per Share

The dividend per share of the OSWC exhibited a fluctuating trend ranging from Rs. 1.75 to Rs. 5.85. Further, the OSWC did not declare dividend during 1990-91 to 1995-96. The average DPS of the Corporation was Rs. 3.81 during the study period.

Dividend Pay-out Ratio

The dividend pay-out ratio of the OSWC revealed a fluctuating trend ranging from 6.48 per cent in 1997-98 to

46.13 per cent in 1989-90. During 1990-91 to 1995-96, the Corporation did not pay any dividend and hence the pay-out ratio was nil. From the study, it is marked that the OSWC retained more profit during later part of the study period to meet its future expansion programme as compared to the initial period.

Profitability Measurement through Du-Pont Approach

The Du-Pont approach is a popular tool of financial analysis. As a useful diagnostic tool, it provides insights into the two determinants of profitability : net profit margin and total assets turnover ratio. The return on investment through Du-Pont model of the OSWC was found to be 2.84% during the study period.

Analysis of Human Resource Performance of the OSWC

The main objective of any organisation is its survival and growth. In order to achieve this objective, the work force engaged in the organisation is responsible. That is, managing the people is the most important aspect of managing the organisation. If the employees put their best efforts then the productivity of the organisation as a whole will be quite high.

The human resources aspect of the OSWC is being governed by the OSWC Staff Regulation, 1985. Basing on it, the recruitment, selection, promotion etc. are being done in the OSWC. The evaluation of human resources performance of the OSWC is made on the basis of the parameters such as income/expenditure per employee, establishment cost per employee, establishment cost per metric ton per employee, capacity utilization per employee etc. The findings of the performance evaluation of human resources are as follows.

Income and Expenditure per Employee

It is found out from the study that in 1985-86 the per employee profit was Rs. 0.13 lakh which was increased to Rs. 0.25 lakh in 1999-2000. Similarly, in the expenditure side, the per employee expenditure during the said period increased from 0.59 lakh in 1985-86 to 2.54 lakh in 1999-2000. Except certain years, the Corporation registered an increasing trend in per employee profit.

Establishment Cost per Employee

It is noticed from the study that the establishment cost per employee was Rs. 14,000 in 1985-86, but over a period of 15 years the same was increased to Rs. 69,000, thus giving about five fold increase in the per employee establishment cost. The study also reveals that the increase in the per employee establishment cost was due to induction of more employees in certain years.

Establishment Cost per Metric Ton

It is observed that the establishment cost per MT in 1985-86 was only Rs. 28.33 and the same was increased to Rs. 161.62 during 1999-2000 which resulted more than 5 times increase. This is mainly due to the increase in the maintenance cost of the warehouses.

Capacity Utilization per Employee

The capacity utilization per employee of the OSWC showed a fluctuating trend throughout the study period. In the year 1985-86 the per employee capacity utilization was 508.38 MT and then it increased to 745.55 MT in 1987-88 and again reduced to 434.52 MT in 1999-2000. The reduction in figure was due to the induction of additional employees during the later part of the study period.

Sources of Income per Employee

It is found from the study that during early part of the study period the income from storage charges ranged from 53 per cent to 68 per cent of the total income. However, during the later part of the study period the income from storage charges reduced considerably, and the income from handling and transportation charges increased and remained within the range of 51 per cent to 57 per cent of the total income. Further, it is noticed from the study that the per employee income of the OSWC was Rs. 71,547 in 1985-86. The same increased to Rs. 2,79,008 in 1999-2000 resulting in an increase of about 4 times during the study period. From the sources of income, it is noteworthy to mention that the storage charge alone cannot take the entire burden of the organization.

Assessment on Reorganisation of Staff Strength in Different Zones

It is observed from the study that the man-power requirement of the OSWC needs redeployment in different zones. The zones namely Cuttack, Berhampur and Balasore have surplus staff. Similarly, the zones like Bhawanipatna, Titilagarh and Sambalpur have shortage of staff. Therefore, to have a rational distribution of staff, redeployment is necessary. This will bring an equilibrium in staffing in one hand and optimum utilisation of warehousing facilities on the other hand.

Testing of Hypotheses

1. *The Orissa State Warehousing Corporation Plays a Vital Role in the Development of the Economy of Orissa.*

The OSWC is a statutory public sector undertaking. The main function of the OSWC is to provide storage facilities to the agricultural and allied produce. To provide storage facilities, it has constructed its own godowns in different parts of the state. Besides, it is also hiring the private godowns to accommodate the surplus stock. It has provided storage facilities to the tune of 2.40 lakh MT during 1999-2000 as against 1.91 lakh MT in 1990-91. In other words, within a decade, it has created additional capacity of 0.49 lakh MT to its existing capacity. Apart from storage facilities, it also renders handling and transportation services to its customers at nominal rate. By discharging the above activities the OSWC has established itself as a premier public sector organisation in the state in the field of scientific storage reducing the post-harvest losses in foodgrains considerably. Due to its network of godown facilities all over the state the farmers are not compelled to sell their produce soon after the harvesting of crops which has enhanced the bargaining power of the farmers and thus, saved them from distress sales. On the basis of warehouse receipts obtained against the produce stored in the godowns of the OSWC, the farmers are getting credit from nationalized banks which has increased their retaining power and enabled them to wait till fair prices are promised for their produce. The OSWC is also engaged in itself in the procurement of foodgrains through the FCI and distribution of essential commodities in the remote areas thus helping the State Government for speedy implementation of its policies for the rural masses. That apart the OSWC has provided direct and indirect employment opportunities to the people of Orissa. The OSWC is contributing revenue regularly to the exchequer of the State Government for the development of State's economy. From the above discussion, it is very clear that the OSWC is playing an important role in the economy of Orissa. Hence, the above hypothesis holds good in the present study.

2. The Orissa State Warehousing Corporation Plays a Leading Role in Providing Storage Facilities in Orissa.

The total foodgrains production in the state is about 70 lakh MT. As against the production, the procurement target fixed by the State Government is 15 lakh MT. The total storage facilities available in the state to accommodate the foodgrains and other notified items is about 6.00 lakh MT taking all public sector organizations like the Food Corporation of India, the Central Warehousing Corporation and the State Warehousing Corporation into account. The total capacity of storage structures of the OSWC available in the state is 2.40 lakh MT which is about 40 per cent of the total available capacity. That apart, out of 30 districts in the state, the OSWC has established 63 warehouses in important locations covering 27 districts. Further, it provides scientific storage facilities for better post-harvest management in the state. From the above discussion it is concluded that the above hypothesis of the study holds good.

3. The Income of the Orissa State Warehousing Corporation is Mainly Dependent upon the Own Capacity and the Occupancy Position of its Warehouses.

The income of the OSWC depends mainly on the capacity and occupancy position of its warehouses. It is seen from the analysis of storage capacity and its utilization that in the initial period of the study the percentage of occupancy was 111 per cent when the profit of the OSWC was Rs. 34.60 lakh. However, due to reduction in the percentage of occupancy particularly during the years from 1990-91 to 1993-94 the OSWC incurred heavy losses. During this period though the own capacity had increased considerably as compared to the initial period, the proportionate increase in occupancy could not be achieved for which the Corporation sustained losses consecutively for a period of 4 years. In the later years when the Coropration concentrated much in constructing its own godowns and reduced dependence on private godowns the occupancy position improved and it resulted higher income in the subsequent years of the study period. Thus, it can be concluded that increase in own capacity and occupancy of the warehouses is one of the main contributing factors for generating income of the Corporation. Hence, the above hypothesis holds true in our study.

4. *The Revenues from Storage and Incidental Charges are Vital for the Survival and Growth of the OSWC.*

The OSWC generates its income largely from storage and incidental (handling and transportation) charges. It is observed from the analysis that during the early part of the study period a sizeable amount of income was derived from the storage component which ranged from 53 per cent to 68 per cent of the total income. However, in the later part the handling and transportation charges contributed significantly and remained within the range of 51 per cent to 57 per cent of the total income. The average income from storage as well as handling and transportation charges were 49.62 per cent and 50.39 per cent respectively which envisaged that neither storage nor income from incidental charges is sufficient enough to meet different obligations of the Corporation. It is, therefore, clear that both income from storage and incidental charges are the vital components for the survival and growth of the OSWC. From the above discussion, it can be concluded that the above hypothesis of the study holds good.

Suggestion

After making an in-depth study on the working of the OSWC, the following suggestions are provided to further improve its performance.

1. As compared to foodgrains production in the state the storage capacity of the OSWC is considered inadequate. Immediate action is to be initiated for construction of additional storage godowns to meet the growing need of the state.

2. The Corporation should give much importance to its godown construction programme rather than depending on hiring of godowns. Further, emphasis on construction should be given in the potential pockets of the state like Bargarh, Sambalpur, Bolangir, Kantabanji, Khariar Road, Nuapada, Bhawanipatna, Junagarh and Dharmagarh etc.

3. Indepth market survey is required to assess the necessity of godowns based on the requirement of depositors of the OSWC especially in the uncovered areas.

4. Apart from storage and related activities, the OSWC should diversify its activities in other potential areas and accordingly evolve the business strategy taking into account the post-liberalisation business scenario.

5. Instead of depending upon one or two major depositors, the OSWC should attract variety of depositors to its business fold. To achieve this, the Corporation should make the tariff rates competitive and reasonable.

6. Government should give support to the OSWC for its business by awarding storage and handling of commodities handled on government-assisted programmes.

7. Rendering qualitative service is the need of the hour. The OSWC should give more emphasis on quality service

to compete with private entrepreneurs in the present liberalized era.

8. Instead of depending solely on its own capital, the OSWC should initiate action to invest more amount in the business by taking long-term loan from the financial institutions. This would give the leverage advantage to the Corporation.

9. The Farmers Extension Service Scheme (FESS) and Disinfestation Service Scheme (DESS) should be popularized among the farmers, traders and others. These schemes will benefit both the OSWC and the customers.

10. The need for developing cost-effective post-harvest technology relevant to the conditions of the different regions has to be given proper attention. This will reduce further the waste and losses in the preservation of foodgrains.

11. Training/orientation programmes should be conducted at regular intervals to make the employees skilled, effective and productive.

12. Modernization and mechanization may be introduced in a phased manner to reduce the dependence of rural labour.

13. Workers participation in management should be encouraged to achieve the common organizational goal.

Practical Utility of the Study

The present study as a whole is a fact-finding research work on the performance evaluation of the OSWC. The study examined the physical, financial and human resources performance of the OSWC through different tools and techniques. This piece of work has the relevance in number of ways to various agencies who are directly or indirectly associated with the working of the OSWC. The management of the organization can utilize the findings of the study to remove the bottlenecks in physical, financial and human resource areas and thereby improve the performance of the organization. In the era of liberalization and privatization, the government can take suitable policy decisions with regard to merger, acquisition, takeover, and diversification etc. of the organization on the basis of the findings of the study. The CWC as a elder partner of the OSWC, can give proper guidance to the OSWC in its functioning on the basis of the findings of the study. The financial institutions and banks while deploying their resources in the organization can evaluate the performance and act accordingly. Last but not the least, the present study is an addition to the existing literature on the working of warehousing organization and the scholars who are working in this area will be immensely benefited by it.

Further Extension of the Study

We have made every attempt to make the study comprehensive but due to the lack of time and resources, there exists certain drawbacks in the scope of the present study. Hence, further research work may be undertaken to overcome the same and enhance the scope of the study. The present study is based on a single unit/organization, i.e., the OSWC. However, its performance has not been compared to any other State Warehousing Corporations. Thus, no inter-firm comparison is made. So, a neighboring State Warehousing Corporation may be included in the extended research work to make it a comparative analysis. This would reveal the strength and weakness of the organization. The data for the study have been mostly collected from secondary source. A more meaningful and useful study can be made if more and more information are collected from primary source. This would help also in getting a clear picture on the working of the OSWC at the field level. The analysis on various aspects made in this study is carried out through simple financial and statistical techniques. However, sophisticated techniques like regression model etc. may be used to enhance the quality of the analysis. On the whole, the present study is just a base upon which a lot more work can be undertaken.

Bibliography

BOOKS

Ackerman, B.K., *Practical Handbook of Warehousing*, The Traffic Service Corporation, Washington, 1986.

Anthony, R.N., *Management Accounting – Text and Cases*, Richard D. Irwin Inc., Homewood, Illinois, 1964.

Anthony, R.N. and Reece, J.S., *Management Accounting-Principles*, Richard D. Irwin Inc., Illinios, 1975.

Atrill, P. and Mclaney, E., *Accounting and Finance for Non-Finance Specialists*, Prentice-Hall of India Pvt. Ltd., New Delhi 1998.

Batty, J., *Management Accountancy*, Macdonald and Evans Ltd., London, 1963.

Bernstein, L.A., *Analysis of Financial Statements*, Richard D. Irwin Inc., Illinois, 1984.

Bhalla, V.K., *Financial Management and Policy*, Anmol Publication Pvt. Ltd., New Delhi, 1998.

Bhat, S.A., *Management of Public Enterprises*, Anmol Publication, New Delhi, 1991.

Burton, G. and Thakur, M., *Management Today - Principles and Practice*, Tata McGraw-Hill Publishing Company Ltd., New Delhi, 1996.

Burton, J.A., *Effective Warehousing*, Macdonald and Evans Ltd., Estover, Ply mouth, 1979.

Chandra, P., *Financial Management – Theory and Practice*, Tata McGraw-Hill Publishing Company Ltd, New Delhi, 1984.

Chandra, P., *Manager's Guide to Finance and Accounting*, Tata-McGraw- Hill Publishing Co., New Delhi, 1985.

Chatterjee, B., *Human Resource Management – A Contemporary Text*, Sterling Publishers Pvt. Ltd., New Delhi, 1996.

Cherunilam, F., *Strategic Management – A Book on Business Policy and Corporate Planning*, Himalaya Publishing House, 1998.

Chhiber, O.N., *Warehousing Corporation in India*, Central Warehousing Corporation, New Delhi, 1982.

Datt, R. and Sundharam, K.P.M., *Indian Economy*, S. Chand and Co. Ltd., New Delhi, 2000.

Dean, J., *Managerial Economics*, Wiley Estern Ltd., New Delhi, 1968.

Dewing, A.S., *The Financial Policy of Corporations*, Ronald Press Company, New York, 1953.

Elhance, D.N., *Fundamentals of Statistics*, Kitab Mahal, Allahabad, 1974.

Foster, G., *Financial Statement Analysis*, Prentice- Hall, Inc., Englewood Cliffs, New Jersey, 1978.

Foulke, R.A., *Practical Financial Statement Analysis*, McGraw Hill Book Company, New York, 1957.

Ghosh, B., *Personnel Management and Industrial Relations*, World Press, Calcutta, 1993.

Gilchrist, R.R., *Managing for Profit: The Added Value Concept*, George Allen and Unwin Ltd., Lodon, 1971.

Gole, V.L., *Fitzgerald's Analysis and Interpretation of Financial Statements*, Butter Worths, 1966.

Graham, B and McGlorik, C., *The Interpretation of Financial Statements*, Harper and Row, New York, 1964.

Gupta, M.C., *Profitability Analysis : An Emprical Approach*, Pointer Publishers, Jaipur, 1989.

Gupta, R.K., Profitability, Financial Structure and Liquidity, Printwell Publishers, Jaipur, 1990.

Gupta, S.P., *Statistical Methods*, Sultan Chand and Sons., New Delhi, 1979.

Hingorani, N.L. and Ramanathan, A.R., *Management Accounting*, Sultan Chand and Sons, New Delhi, 1973.

Hingorani, N.L., Ramanathan, A.R. and Grewal, T.S., *Management Accounting*, Sultan Chand and Sons, New Delhi, 1977.

Howard, B.B. and Upton, M., *Introduction to Business Finance*, McGraw Hill Book Company, New York, 1953.

Hunt, P., Williams, H. and Donaldson, G., *Basic Business Finance-Text and Cases*, Richard D. Irwin, Illinois, 1966.

Kaveri, V.S., *Financial Ratios as Predictors of Borrower's Health with Special Reference to Small Scale Industries in India*, Sultan Chand and Sons, New Delhi, 1980.

Kennedy, R.D. and McMullen, S.Y., *Financial Management-Form, Analysis and Interpretations*, Richard D. Irwin, Inc., Illinois, 1968.

Khan, M.Y. and Jain, P.K., *Financial Management*, Tata McGraw-Hill Publishing Company Ltd, New Delhi, 1982.

Kothari, C.R., *Research Methodology – Methods and Techniques*, Vishwa Prakashan, New Delhi, 1990.

Kristen, M.M., *Corporation Finance – An Introduction to Principle and Practices*, Harper and Row, New York, 1975.

Kuchhal, S.C., *Financial Management – An Analytical and Conceptual Approach*, Chaitanya Publishing House, Allahabad, 1977.

Kulkarni, P.V., *Business Finance : Principles and Problems*, Himalaya Publishing House, Bombay, 1988.

Kulshrestha, N.K., *Analysis of Financial Statement of Paper Industry in India*, Navman Prakashan, Aligarh, 1972.

Kulshrestha, N.K., *Theory and Practice of Management Accounting*, Navman Prakashan, Aligarh, 1976.

Lee, C.F., *Financial Analysis and Planning-Theory and Application*, Addison Wesley Publishing Company, U.S.A., 1985.

Lev, B., *Financial Statement Analysis – A New Approach*, Prentice-Hall Inc, Englewood Cliffs, New Jersey, 1974.

Mackinnon, J.A. and Troupe, L.J.E., *Accounts Analysis*, Gee and Company (Publishers) Ltd, London, 1948.

Maheshwari, S.N., *Financial and Cost Accounting*, Sultan Chand and Sons, New Delhi, 2000.

Mathur, B.L., *Financial Management in Public Enterprises,* RBSA Publishers, Jaipur, 1987.

Mishra, S.K. and Puri, V.K., *Indian Economy – It's Development Experience,* Himalaya Publishing House, New Delhi, 2001.

Moore, C.L., *Managerial Accounting,* Anold Publishers Ltd., London, 1961.

Nair, N.G. and Nair, L., *Personnel Management and Industrial Relations,* S. Chand and Co. Ltd, New Delhi, 2001.

Pandey, I.M., *Financial Management,* Vikas Publishing House Pvt. Ltd., New Delhi, 1994.

Powell, G. V., *Warehousing - Analysis for Effective Operations,* Communica Europa, London, 1976.

Prakash, O.M., *Ratio Analysis of Management in New Perspective – Management Ratios,* Himalaya Publishing House, Bombay, 1987.

Sahay, S.N., *Financial Management of Public Enterprises,* Sultan Chand and Co., New Delhi, 1984.

Sharma, R.K. and Gupta, S.K., *Management Accounting-Principles and Practice,* Kalyani Publishers, New Delhi, 1983.

Sharma, S.C., *Warehousing and Distribution – A Study in Agro Industrial Development,* Uma Publication, New Delhi, 1986.

Shukla, M.B., *Profitability Management in Public Enterprises,* Tiwari Publication, New Delhi, 1991.

Singh, J. and Paul, R., *Management Accounting,* Kitab Mahal, Allahabad, 1982.

Soloman, E. and Pringle, J.J., *An Introduction to Financial Management,* Prentice Hall of India Pvt. Ltd, New Delhi, 1978.

Srivastava, R.M., *Financial Management and Policy,* Himalaya Publishing House, New Delhi, 1997.

Weston, J.F. and Brigham, E.F., *Manageiral Finance,* Holt, Rinehart and Winston, New York, 1969.

JOURNALS

Arora, B.K. and Raju, K.V.R., "Rural Godowns - Where they have failed and how they can Succeed", *Agricultural Marketing*, Vol. XXXIV, No.1, 1991.

Asthana, M.D. Bansal, R.N., and Jain, M.C., "Improving Technical Efficiency in Food Marketing", *Agricultural Marketing*, Vol. XXXIX, No. 2, July - September, 1996.

Bangal, S.S., "Reaching remote areas thro' revamped PDS", *Kurukshetra*, Vol. XL, No. 8, May, 1992.

Bhatia, G.R., "Agricultural Marketing in India - Some Important Issues", *Agricultural Marketing*, Vol. XXXI, No. 3, October-December, 1988.

Bhatia, G.R., "Agricultural Marketing Research, Surveys and Planning in India", *Agricultural Marketing*, Vol. XXXII, No. 2, July-September, 1989.

Bhuyan, Sanjib., "State Intervention in Agricultural Marketing: Is it necessary", *Agricultural Marketing*, Vol. XXXIII, No. 1, April-June, 1990.

Biwas, P.K. and Parasher, M.P., "Development of Agricultural Produce Markets in India", *Agricultural Marketing*, Vol. XXXIII, No. 2, July-September, 1990.

Choyal, B.R., "Pricing in Public Sector : Problems of Pricing in CWC", *Indian Management*, Vol. 21, No. 12, December, 1982.

Gill, K.S., Sidhu, D.S. and Sidhu, M.S., "Storage losses of Foodgrains at farm level in Punjab", *Agricultural Marketing*, Vol. XXX, No. 4, January-March, 1988.

Gurumoorthy T.R., "Public Distribution System-a Boon for Rural People", *Kurukshetra*, Vol. XL, No. 8, May, 1992.

Krishna, and Gururaj., "Warehousing Corporation : Task Ahead....", *www.CommodityIndia.com.*, Vol. I, Issue 6, August 2001.

Paramasivam, K.M., "Market Planning-Techniques and Methodology for drawing out Master Plan", *Agricultural Marketing*, Vol. XXVIII, No. 2, July-September, 1985.

Pattnaik, B.B., "Role of Public Warehousing in Agricultural Marketing" *CWC News,* Vol. II, No. 4, July-August, 1992.

Randhawan, N.S., "Indian Agriculture - Extent and Direction of Progress", *Yojana,* Vol. XXI, Nos. 14 and 15, August 15, 1987.

Ranganathan, A., "Warehousing Corporation - A Profile", *Yojana,* Vol. XXX, No. 20, November 1-15, 1986.

Satish, S.V. and Indira, M., "Post Harvest : In need of Face lift," *www.comodityindia.com.,* Vol. I, Issue 7, September 2001.

Singh, H.P. and Saxena, B.S., "Problems in Classification of Rice and Formulation in its Grade Specification in India", *Agricultural Marketing,* Vol. XXXI, No. 4, Januray-March, 1989.

Sri Ram, T.V., "Improvement of Storage Condition and Storage Methods in India," *Productivity,* Vol. XIV, No. 4, January-March, 1974.

Subba Rao, N.V., "Functioning of Agricultural Market Committees in Andhra Pradesh", *Agricultural Marketing,* Vol. XXIX, No. 3, October - December, 1986.

Thomas, P.M., "Management of Storage, Preservation, Transportation and Processing Foodgrains in India", *Productivity,* Vol. XIV, No. 4, January-March, 1974.

Upendra, M., "Marketing Behaviour of Farmers - A study at Farm Level," *Agricultural Marketing,* Vol. XXXIII, No. 2, July-September, 1990.

REPORTS AND MANUALS

A Project Report on Manpower Assessment in the OSWC, 2000, Social Enrichment Workers' Association, Bhubaneswar.

Annual Financial Statement, Finanance Department, Government of Orissa, 2001-2002.

Annual Report, Department of Agriculture and Co-operation, Government of India, 1997-98.

Annual Reports, Department of Food and Public Distribution, Government of India, 1999-2000 and 2000-2001.

Annual Reports, Central Warehousing Corporation, New Delhi, 1985-86 to 1999-2000.

Annual Reports, Orissa State Warehousing Corporation, Bhubaneswar, 1985-86 to 1999-2000.

Economic Survey, Government of India, 1997-98.

Gramin Vikas Newsletter, Department of Rural Development, Government of India, June, 1990.

Gramin Vikas Newsletter, Department of Rural Development, Government of India, January, 1990.

Orissa Agricultural Statistics, Directorate of Agriculture and Food Production, Government of Orissa, 2000.

Orissa State Warehousing Corporation Staff Regulation, Notification, The 10th July 1985, The Orissa Gazettee, 1985.

Public Enterprises Profile for Financial year 1992-93 and 1995-96, Government of Orissa.

Report of Comptroller and Auditor General of India for the year ended 31st March, 1998, Government of Orissa.

Report on Cenesus of India, Directorate of Census Operations, Bhubaneswar, Orissa, 2001.

Save Grain Manual, Government of India, New Delhi, 1990.

Souvenir Published on Silver Jubilee of Orissa State Warehousing Corporation, 1958-83, Bhubaneswar, 1983.

Study material on *Human Resource Management and Human Resource Utilisation,* Department of General Administration, Gopabandhu Academy, Government of Orissa, August, 1999.

System, Procedure and Practices of Scientific Storage, Vol. I and II, CWC, New Delhi, 1982.

The Warehousing Corporations Act, 1962.

Warehousing News, Central Warehousing Corporation, New Delhi, October-December, 1978.

Index